A TIME FOR WHITE ROSES

A TIME FOR WHITE ROSES

Dorris June Brannon

Copyright © 2000 by Dorris June Brannon.

ISBN #:   Softcover   0-7388-3257-X

All rights reserved. No part of this book may be reproduced or transmitted in any form or by any means, electronic or mechanical, including photocopying, recording, or by any information storage and retrieval system, without permission in writing from the copyright owner.

This book was printed in the United States of America.

To order additional copies of this book, contact:
Xlibris Corporation
1-888-7-XLIBRIS
www.Xlibris.com
Orders@Xlibris.com

CONTENTS

PREFACE 9
CHAPTER ONE 15
CHAPTER TWO 27
CHAPTER THREE 38
CHAPTER FOUR 50
CHAPTER FIVE 62
CHAPTER SIX 76
CHAPTER SEVEN 87
CHAPTER EIGHT 96
CHAPTER NINE 107
CHAPTER TEN 118
CHAPTER ELEVEN 138
CHAPTER TWELVE 152
CHAPTER THIRTEEN 162
CHAPTER FOURTEEN 174
CHAPTER FIFTEEN 179

EPILOGUE 191

*This book is lovingly dedicated to
Mother and Anamary
—wherever they are—
and to the Doctor Annies of the world
who are brave enough to also be humane.*

PREFACE

There is a kind of presumption basic to all literary effort—namely, that the writer has something of value to say—but an autobiography takes the presumption a step further by implying that he has something of value to say about himself. It would seem that humility is inherently inimical to such an undertaking, yet this work is offered in just such a spirit. It is not I, but certain circumstances of my life quite beyond my control, that I feel worthy of commemoration in this fashion. To the extent that they represent variations on universal themes of the human condition, they may serve to instruct as well as comfort others.

Purists, accustomed in our electronic age to tight plots wedged in between television commercials, may object to evidence that I have meandered a bit in the telling of my tale, but life does not happen in neat sequences. The shortest distance between birth and death is seldom a straight line. The path twists and turns, forcing us to stop now and then to check on our bearings and reflect upon how we have arrived where we are. That is how I have approached *A Time for White Roses,* relying heavily upon Mark Twain's formula for writing an autobiography:

> Start it at no particular time in your life; wander at your free will all over your life; talk only about the thing which interests you for the moment: drop it the moment its interest threatens to pale, and turn your talk upon the new and more interesting thing that has intruded itself into your mind meantime. . . .

His attempts at a formal autobiography based upon straightforward chronology were inevitably pitched as being too dry and lifeless, and, in a similar vein, Twain's contemporary Robert Louis Stevenson once complained of trying to keep a journal that his efforts in that regard always tended towards mere posturing. Those two hazards are the Scylla and Charybdis of reporting one's own experiences. I hope I have avoided both. If not, my apologies are tendered in advance.

Some notable aspects of my history are conspicuous in their absence. For example, I have deliberately omitted details of three marriages that ended in divorce. For the most part, they contributed only tangentially to progress towards a satisfactory appreciation of my role in the "scheme of things" and are better left to the imagination. It is because of them, however, that I have chosen to use my maiden name as a pseudonym. Not all my children have the same surnames, and I am reluctant to appear partial by using one as opposed to another.

The astute reader will soon conclude that there is more going on here than a straightforward memoir, since *A Time for White Roses* is laced with incidental observations ranging from bemused candor and sober philosophy to rather strident soapbox opinion and daring speculation. But of what value is a life lived that does not draw from experience an evolving assessment of everything that has contributed to its development? It is not so much what one does that is meaningful to succeeding generations, but what one has learned as a result. It is my earnest belief that ordinary people are quite capable of reading and understanding a work that doesn't fit neatly into most publishers' well-defined notions of genre. On the strength of that faith, I have refused to make *Roses* conform strictly to any number of editors' demands for its revision. Whether I will be vindicated or not remains to be seen.

It would be impossible to thank everyone whose encouragement has played a role over the last several years in launching *A Time for White Roses*. Some friends stand out, however, and must be given grateful recognition, even though the object of their support was not timely realized. In alphabetical order, they are Dr. John Bierk, Gerald Brother, Dan Fredman, Marcia Griffith, Darcy Mullhaupt Dillon, Dr. John Thomas Richards, and Charles L. Tanberg. Each of them knows the unique and invaluable contribution he or she made and is entitled to bask vicariously in whatever acclaim this book may eventually enjoy. Additional help came from yet another source which, sadly enough, cannot be made public. It can only be hoped that, in years to come, this benefactor, reluctant after the fact to have been a party to an effort he regards as misguided, will finally forgive me any displeasure my interpretation of life has brought him.

May any toes I tread upon mend well and quickly and any windows I chance to open in the occasional closed mind remain forever open.

Finally, I want to thank Bertie Austin Brannon in memoriam for violating the best conventional wisdom, and making it possible for me to grow up as

Dorris June Brannon.
June 22, 2000 (Sara's tenth birthday)
Portland, Oregon

We have come from Jerusalem, where we found not what we sought.

> Spoken by disembodied spirits heard in chorus by Carl G. Jung and recorded in *Septem Sermones*

... so far as the element of separation is concerned ... to spirit there are no bounds, and ... spiritual communion, whether between two persons in the body or two persons, one in the body and one out of the body, is within reach of all. In the degree that the higher spiritual life is realized can there be this higher spiritual communion.

> From *In Tune With the Infinite*
> —Ralph Waldo Trine

... never dance to anyone's tune if it doesn't entirely content you.

> From a letter to Lionardo di Buonarroto
> —Michelangelo

The immortal and eternal Being in us forever summons knowledge, eternal science, as an aim of its fleeting incarnation as man's duty.

> From *The Egyptian Miracle: An Introduction to the Wisdom of the Temple*
> —R.A. Schwaller de Lubicz

Mechanical movement is the energy of despair, the revolt of Spirit against its entrapment within determination.

> *Ibid.*

... harmony is essentially Number, for it is the disposition that, within certain given conditions, cannot be otherwise.

> *Ibid.*

CHAPTER ONE

When I was a small child, a rosebush that had never known the pruner's touch grew by our front porch. It went every which way, unfettered and untamed. As if by magic, its first buds never failed to open just in time for Mother's Day. I watched them every year with an anxious and vigilant eye, for they were all I had to give my mother when her day rolled around. Early on those designated May Sundays, I would brave the thorns while they still dripped dew; then clutching my somewhat mauled bouquet and beaming my best smile, I would deliver it into my mother's hands. As surely as the day came and the roses bloomed, she always buried her face in their velvet crimson and said wistfully, "When I was young, it was a custom on Mother's Day to wear a red rose if your mother was living or a white one if she was not." Her own mother had died only two days before I was three.

I was too young then to understand why my present seemed to make her sad, to comprehend the magnitude of her recent loss. Now my time has come to wear white roses, and now I understand. In the immediate aftermath of her death, the only adequate articulation I could give my sense of devastation was "I want to go home, and there's no place to go." Never before had I realized to what an extent *home* and *mother* are, and were intended by Nature to be, synonymous. She had lived with me the last ten years of her life; therefore, it wasn't a material location for which I yearned, an environment in which I could revive memories of times long past. It was, instead, an intangible safety net for the heart; a state of belonging, of knowing and being known; a condition of permitted trial and forgiven error, each balanced on a scale called *love*. It was a private and unique lexicon by which I defined *self*—a definition that began disintegrating as the language slipped beyond command like a melody maddeningly out of the mind's reach.

I have lost others whose lives went a long way toward shaping mine, but none of those losses created the terrible inner void left in the wake of Mother's death. These relative consequences are not so natural as the textbook psychologist might smugly suggest. Their genesis is, in fact, rather complicated. They reflect the warp and woof of a bizarre and remarkable destiny which I can only contemplate now with awe and humble gratitude. In that intricate mesh of interwoven events is a tale that demands to be told. If others can find in its pattern a hidden thread of meaning common to all from which they can weave a new appreciation of life, my *raison d'etre* will have been fulfilled.

I enter the story in 1935. America was then crawling out of an economic abyss while Europe teetered on the brink of a different and even more horrifying plunge. The Great Depression—or "The Crash" as my family always referred to it—still cast a ghastly pall across the country. Typical of the "poor who got poorer" during that period, Bert and Gracie Brannon lost their modest but comfortable home to a bank foreclosure. Laid off indefinitely from his job on the railroad, Bert could find nothing else to do. Humiliated and desperate, the couple had no recourse but to fall back upon such charity as Gracie's five Frank brothers and some faithful friends could offer. These all lived within the radius of a few miles from one another on hilly farms near Dexter, Missouri, to the north and west of the Bootheel.

The second oldest Frank boy, Wilson—soon to be dead of multiple sclerosis—deeded them a parcel of his land on which stood a small but sturdy clapboard structure intended for use as a woodshed. With the little they had salvaged from better times and the wealth of ingenuity peculiar to their kind, they converted this shack into what Mother always called "the doll house." Left frail and sickly from childhood malaria and, in all probability, rheumatic fever, she fully expected to curl up and die there, if not from deprivation, then certainly from shame. She was denied fulfillment of so theatrical a demise, however, tailored to her temporary state of despair. Fresh air and hard work and the human necessity of finding pleasure in small things like bright cretonne curtains and large ones like love transformed her into a new person, stronger than she had ever been and happier during this difficult interval than she would profess to be again.

Though the Brannons had already been married fifteen years in 1935, they still remained childless. One miscarriage was as close as Gracie would ever come to maternity in the strict medical sense of that term. She and Bert had visited orphanages from time to time, window-shopping as it were. Occasionally a tiny hand had to be pried loose from one of theirs, taking with it great aching chunks of heart, but they hesitated to make a final commitment to parenthood. There loomed the specter of Gracie's uncertain health—that and the nagging possibility of taking a child with some irremediable flaw of character, popularly believed to be hereditary through some mysterious process by which many held that immorality taints the blood.

Adoption in those days was widely regarded as falling somewhere between having an unmentionable disease at best and courting potential disaster at worse. Genteel folk had the good taste and manners never to discuss it openly with the principals involved. Many adopted children (not that there were many in 1935) discovered their transplanted roots—if they did at all—only by virtue of blundering Cousin Somebody's slip of the tongue or the deliberate malice of a disgruntled playmate, maybe one living next door to the gossiping neighborhood archivist whose perennial business is always recording and publicizing other people's.

Sometime during the summer of 1934, Gracie's oldest brother stopped by on his way to Poplar Bluff, twenty-seven miles southwest of Dexter, to ask if Bert would like to accompany him. Walter—known to everyone as JW or Jay Walter (his first name was James)—owned the only automobile in the Frank clan and shared its use generously. Bert jumped at the chance to see whether any job opportunities had opened up since his last inquiry.

Poplar Bluff was the largest rail center on the Missouri-Pacific Lines between Saint Louis and Little Rock. Coupling boxcars shook floors and rattled windows many blocks from the switching yards, and soot from belching steam engines constituted the housewife's greatest challenge. Linoleums that had been laboriously scrubbed and waxed to a shine in the morning would turn bare feet black on the bottom long before the day was up, and no matter how passionately a child pleaded the case for mere permanent stain, these same bare feet always ended up having to be washed at bedtime. Whistles of the responsible behemoths, forever arriving and departing, frequently halted conversation at a considerable remove. Holding the thought was thus a way of life in a significant part of the community—on both sides of the track—and promoted a patience only slightly less remarkable, let's say, than that required of Trappist monks.

It so happened that Jay Walter's errand in the Bluff that day took him and Bert to the vicinity of the Smith Hospital, where Gracie had been treated from time to time. The two-story building, covered with yellow brick, asbestos siding as I recall, was actually more a clinic than a hospital. The facility was owned and operated by a husband-and-wife team of osteopaths, called "Dr. Joe" and "Dr. Annie" for obvious reasons. Their practice reflected the prevailing mores: he saw all the male patients, she all the female.

The medical community—that is, the MDs—had not yet welcomed osteopaths into the fold, despite their standard medical and surgical qualifications. It was therefore, no doubt, a combination of professional malevolence and personal spite that made Dr. Annie the target of attempts to have her license revoked on the grounds of a widespread rumor that she performed abortions. Her gender was an added onus, of course. She had presumed to intrude upon a sacred male domain from which they would have liked to expel her in ignominy. It could never be legally established that she was guilty as charged, however, so the medical physicians had no choice but to withdraw in sullen defeat, keeping a mute but watchful truce.

What they and everyone else had no trouble seeing was that Doctor Annie took pregnant young women—unmarried pregnant young women—under her wing, giving them refuge in the hospital for as long as it was necessary. If they could not afford to pay for their room and board (and few indeed could), they performed menial tasks to earn it—tasks like wrapping bandages and sterilizing instruments or doing light housekeeping work. When the infants Dr. Annie delivered them of were not wanted, she personally sought homes for them, sending them to the nearest orphanage only as an unpleasant last resort. To avoid this, she even kept some herself, rearing them along with her own brood of offspring.

Many years after Dr. Annie's death, I was invited to show some of my paintings at a dinner meeting of the Southeast Missouri Medical Association in Cape Girardeau. During the preliminary cocktail hour, I chanced to meet an elderly osteopath and asked him point blank if the old rumor about her was true. He laughed heartily and said, "You bet! I cleaned up some of the messes she left!"

As I told him, I was one of the messes she didn't get to soon enough. By turns, I have been both sorry and glad about that. The point is, though, that performing abortions in a day when opportunities for women in general were limited and even men were standing in bread lines was but another facet of Dr. Annie's humanitarian nature. Aside from the financial difficulties arising from pregnancy out of wedlock, there was still the element of disgrace to overcome prior to World War II, and it was no small hurdle to clear, not only for the unfortunate mother, but her child as well. Birth certificates of bastards in many states were stamped "Illegitimate," a record that followed them to their death. Rather than turn this into a diatribe on the subject, I simply recommend that all doubting Thomases peruse John Irving's pertinent and candid novel (now also a movie) *The Cider House Rules*.

Knowing about Dr. Annie's custom of caring for unwed mothers, Bert Brannon, on a sudden whim that morning in Poplar Bluff, threw his yearning to be a father squarely into the lap of Fate and dropped by her office to make a request. Would she let him know if a baby girl with black hair became available for adoption? Absolutely, she would, and gladly.

Months went by, and there was still no work. The incident was all but forgotten in the daily struggle for survival. The winter was harsh, and Gracie wept once over a pan of biscuits burned beyond human—and even canine—consumption. Small miracles, by the same token, produced great happiness. Desperately needing shoes, Bert made five dollars one night pulling a car out of a mud hole with his team of horses. The unexpected and unsolicited reward amounted precisely to the cost of new footwear.

Then one cold February morning the carrier left a strange, unsigned postcard in the Brannons' mailbox. Gracie read its cryptic content and was mystified. "Come to Poplar Bluff," it said, "prepared to do some shopping. Your order is ready for delivery." She wrapped her shawl tightly around her thin shoulders and went to the barn, where Bert was feeding the horses. But not the cow. They did not own a cow.

"What in the world is this?" she asked, handing him the card.

Her husband took one look and gave a yell.

"We have a baby!" he shouted gleefully.

"You're crazy!" she protested, incredulous. "We can't even afford to feed ourselves, much less a baby!"

But Bert was not to be dissuaded by mere practicality. His response was emphatic.

"If we were going to have one of our own," he argued, "we'd go ahead and have it."

And that was that. It may have been the only time in his married life that he asserted his authority with such finality.

"I'm going over to borrow Jay Walter's car," he went on, already saddling one of the mares. "You be ready to leave when I get back."

And away he went, leaving Gracie stunned and speechless. But ready she was when he returned, if putting on her best Sunday-go-to-meeting dress and grabbing a quilt off the bed can be called getting ready for what was to follow.

There have been times over the years when it appeared to me that God is really a committee. Or perhaps it's just that the lesser lights overseeing mundane human events can't always agree on what ought and ought not to happen. Right down to the wire, my future seemed to be up for grabs. The youngster dispatched to the train station to post the momentous card announcing my availability mistakenly put it in the southbound mail instead of the northbound, so its delivery to the Brannons was delayed a day. Had they not arrived just when they did, I would have gone, within the very hour, to a doctor in St. Louis.

But they did arrive, and though a bit on the scrawny side and a tab jaundiced, I did have the specified heavy shock of black hair. And I was definitely a girl. What life might have been for me in a more prosperous and medically sophisticated environment makes for interesting, if useless, speculation, but even the rosiest of fantasies leave no room at this point for regret.

My new parents were not permitted to meet the young woman who had so recently borne me, but Gracie contrived to ask her a question through the crack of a door slightly ajar.

"Is there anything you'd like me to name her?" she inquired as a bow to the other's prior claim.

The answer was curt and to the point: "She's yours now. Name her whatever you like."

What manner of pain lay buried beneath that cold indifference can only be surmised, but I am sure she took it to the grave with her. Pro-Life propaganda conveniently glosses over the terrible violence done a normal female's psyche when she consigns her helpless infant to the uncertain care of total strangers—strangers, for all she knows, like the cocaine freak Joel Steinberg, who beat his little adopted daughter to death. Even less extreme and more commonplace events like divorce have a doubly hurtful effect upon adoptees, who have to deal not only with a disrupted home life, but their inner sense of detachment as well.

Can a woman forget her suckling child? Isaiah asks. That unlikelihood is more likely, he implies, than God's irrevocable renunciation of His people. It is the only fitting analogy the prophet could have drawn, the only one that could come even close to expressing the concept of absolute fidelity. The patent difference between a tiny individual whose personhood is an independent and established reality, subject to physical and psychological pain, and a clump of dividing cells incapable of functioning outside the uterus should not warrant so much as a second thought, let alone the bitter and—all too often—bloody debate that rages over abortion. Custom and hospital recommendation have traditionally held against formal interment of naturally aborted embryos and miscarried fetuses until the fifth month of gestation. If they are not considered sufficiently "human" to be named and given burial in the context of a religious ritual, then why are they sufficiently "human" to be considered the victims of "murder"?

Financial duress as well as avoidance of public scandal doubtless influenced my natural mother's decision to give away her child, as it has many another woman's. The supreme irony was that I wound up with people too poor to buy kerosene for their only lamp.

Bringing another human being into the world or contracting to rear one already in existence entails the most awesome and difficult responsibility known to man, yet infants continue to be mere products of recreational lust, of ignorance, of sentimentality, of apathy. Only rarely are they born of love and a desire to express it through propagation. Whatever the occasion of their conception, they did not, as the cliché goes, ask to be born, but there they are, and they grow up into people who have to be reckoned with—often, if their lives have begun and been lived in an environment conducive to crime, ending up in prison or being executed. Most conservatives passionate in their condemnation of abortion have no problem at all condoning murder of adults by state decree, and they also choose to forget that the ovum fertilized as a result of rape is every bit as potentially human as the one fertilized in the best blessed of marriage beds.

At any rate, the woman who is unable or unwilling to assume the burden of maternity has absolutely no business becoming gravid in the first place, as my birth mother did, and any organization calling itself a religion that would impose barriers against safe contraceptive prevention of unwanted pregnancy merely consigns a large portion of the living to that hell it reserves, in principle, for most of the dead.

With my bridges already burning two days into my fragile life, I was blissfully unaware of the complications I introduced to my immediate milieu and was equally unconscious of any disadvantage that accrues from not being "to the manor born." This condition would later provide grist from which valuable insights would be ground. I have learned, for example, that one is not worthy of having a great deal until he has had occasion to be properly grateful for having only a little. It is therefore no matter for embarrassment to me that my first cap and sweater set was made from an aunt's best towel and my diapers from bleached flour sacks. I had only one bottle and one nipple for it, both borrowed from a niece of Mother's who had recently given birth.

As soon as the Brannons returned home with me (virtually suffocated in the depths of my full-sized quilt), Dad hied him over to my new grandmother's to see what she and Mother's sister, Anamary, might have that could be used for a baby. So unexpected was my arrival that the dear old thing asked, "Baby what? Calf?" It was an understandable mistake. Mother's local doctor, on hearing via the grapevine that she had an infant, said with some vehemence, "That can't be! I just saw her two weeks ago, and she was flat as a board, I tell you! Flat as a board!"

The only family member for whom I was not a pleasant surprise was the Brannons' dog, Bruce. He had been pampered as few children are privileged to be. Because he was terrified of thunder, Gracie was known to get up during the night sometimes and escort him to the storm cellar through a raging torrent. That's pretty privileged. Small wonder that his jealousy toward me knew no bounds. He would not enter a room if I was in it, and when held once and forced by Dad to look at me, he turned up his head and howled so pitifully that the introductions were abandoned instantly, and whatever terms he and I were to come to were relegated to Dame Fortune thenceforth.

Flat or rotund, Gracie now embarked upon the joys and sorrows of motherhood at the rather advanced age of forty-four, a time when most women are beginning to savor a bit of relief from the more constant trials and tribulations of child-rearing. Bert was six years younger. It did not ease their burden to learn very shortly that they had no ordinary foundling. As a university student in the 1950s, I fumed at the tripe peddled by Skinner and Watson, who were then riding high on the crest of the always unstable wave of scientific acclaim. I knew very well that we are not merely products of our environment, for hadn't I grown up listening to accounts of my early life that belied their thesis?

For example, it was soon discovered that I came with my taste in music as intact as the color of my hair. The Brannons had managed to hang on to an ante-Depression Victrola. Some records they played—one in particular called "I Told the Stars About You"—lulled me to sleep while others never failed to elicit episodes of fretting that didn't stop till the music did. It therefore became politic not to play records in the dark anymore, a practice they had turned into a guessing game to accommodate their want of kerosene. Then, in spite of being exposed to nothing but country and gospel music for years, I continued to hate both, only finding my true passion as a young adult on first hearing classical works.

I also exhibited other definite preferences. As soon as I had sufficient nubbins of teeth to discover what fun it is to snap rubber nipples, I bit a hole in mine. Funds were eked out for a new one, which I steadfastly refused to accept. As pangs of hunger brought on screams of pain (and probably anger), my dad suggested sewing up the old nipple with needle and thread, but Mother was made of sterner stuff. I had thrown down the gauntlet, and she was not about to concede defeat while she still enjoyed so great an advantage in size. I reportedly held out twenty-four hours without eating—probably setting a record for infantile obstinacy. When the new nipple suffered the same fate, I flatly rejected its replacement and, at only seven months old, weaned myself to a cup. It was still early in the match, and I had won the second round. Some rounds, Mother and I were to discover, would end in a draw.

The only discernibly beautiful thing about poverty is that it brooks no weaklings. The perpetual whiner who *can't* had better be born with a silver spoon in his mouth. Mother met every challenge with an inventive solution. It would have been easy, for instance, to sit home complaining after I became too hefty for her to lift me onto Old Pat for our daily jaunts over to Grandma's. Instead, she put me on a table in the yard with a heavy rock between my legs securing my dress tail, then mounted the mare and rode by for me. One time I watched in innocent glee while she was dragged around the yard with her foot in a stirrup after a paper bag she was holding frightened her mount. Luckily I couldn't yet talk, for she kept the mishap a secret from everyone else, skillfully hiding her bruises and disguising her limps.

Lacking any other way to safely restrain me while she performed her endless household duties, she stood me in a wooden chair frame whose rush bottom was long gone, tying kitchen gadgets to it for my amusement. Consequently, I never crawled, but I did walk alone at nine months, since mastering the art of balance is half the battle in learning that skill.

Eventually Dad was summoned back by MoPac to work on the "extra board," the pool of employees on standby to fill in for absentee regulars. For a while, Mother stayed on to run the farm unaided, but she came up against a fact as old as husbandry: nothing can alter pastoral contentment so effectively as hogs possessed with a desire to forage beyond the confines of their allotted space. The barrier does not exist that will deter such dedication to single-minded purpose. It was Gracie's third fence-mending effort in two days that did the trick. She threw down her hammer, packed our clothes, and turned her back forever on agrarian life. The place was let out to her youngest brother, Marvin, and we joined my father in a rooming house in the small Ozark community of Bismarck. Our accommodations there soon proved to be a very cramped substitute for forty acres, so before long we were settled into a cozy little house in Poplar Bluff.

Had Mother known what was in store, she might have come to some mutual understanding with the hogs—using the hammer on their heads instead of the fence, perhaps—but at nine months I still appeared to be in perfect health. I had a fairly wide vocabulary that included "pretty chicky" (for *parrot*) and "Hello, Thursia," a phrase picked up from hearing it addressed to the telephone frequently. Expectations for my future ran high among all but Dad's father, who said something terrible was going to happen to me because I was "much too intelligent." Whether clean country air could have forestalled the imminent onset of a vicious lung disease is moot, but it's a cinch that the Bluff's ubiquitous coal dust played a major role in hastening its progress. As it turned out, Charlie Brannon was all too right, if arguably for the wrong reason. The Wicked Fairy had the last word, and her curse would cast a lasting blight upon the many gifts bestowed by her more benevolent sisters.

CHAPTER TWO

We are all mosaics, put together randomly it seems, a fragment at a time. Seldom are we privileged to detect the overall pattern, since we are in it and of it. Vital pieces often appear to be missing altogether, so incongruous is the juxtaposition of colors and textures. Mother was at a complete loss to fathom some of the more extreme contradictions inherent in my behavior, my attitude towards water being one of the most puzzling. Baths were nightmares. When a drop of water hit my head, I came up fighting the air and anything in it that got in my way, simultaneously yelling bloody murder. Even in the summertime, she closed all the doors and windows as a prelude to these ordeals lest the neighbors think she was killing me.

Concurrently, I displayed a morbid fascination for submerging other things in that medium—other living things, that is. Two notable instances stand out: unnaturally quiet for too long, I was tracked down at Grandma's and caught in the act of baptizing a whole brood of baby chickens in a tub of rainwater, one by one. Each time, I held my tiny captive under until it blubbered and then carefully stood it on a nearby rock to dry. What a congregation of shivering, cheeping, bedraggled things that was! Their condition brought about my first dose of corporal punishment—a curative Mother was to begin applying as liberally as the drops of turpentine on spoons of sugar that were equally as distasteful. This did not deter me from committing further breaches of the law pertaining to unauthorized christenings, however.

I was still only two when I seized a tomcat by all fours and treated him to the same purification rites. With rare exceptions, cats are notorious for their hatred of water, and this particular feline—black at that—was possessed of a demonic temperament as well. Mother never ceased to marvel that he spared my life. The fact that I was wearing a bonnet saved my face from permanent disfigurement. His dousing was not observed to improve upon his disposition afterwards, but he was observed to stay well beyond range of any further mischief I might have had in mind. I did, in fact, conjure up more. When slightly older, I cut off another cat's whiskers flush with his furry face—God knows why. Maybe just to see how he would look without them. Chastened by Mother to an abject welter of contrition, I patrolled our picket fence for days expecting to find his head stuck, for she had explained to me that cats use their whiskers to measure space: if the whiskers go through a hole, so will the rest of them.

Sage elders predicted that I would outgrow my fear of water, and in time my father attempted to prove them right by taking me swimming with him in the Black River that flows through Poplar Bluff and served in those days as the community's "pool." Mother and Anamary always sat primly on the bank making moues of disapproval regarding the public exposure of so much bare flesh. And this when bikinis were still a gleam in some lecher's eye.

Sometimes on hot, lazy Sunday afternoons, we took our lawn chairs to the river and set them up under spreading shade trees to watch real baptizings. The procedure called for the minister to wade out into the water to a depth of his waist and there place a folded handkerchief over the mouth and nose of the person to be ritually cleansed prior to dunking his new convert. On one such occasion, a woman either got the Spirit or had second thoughts just as she went under. If nothing else, she proved beyond the shadow of a doubt that it is impossible to shout submersed. What a great floundering and splashing ensued! Oh, it was a fine, exciting spectacle! Both baptizer and baptizee appeared in considerable danger of being taken to Abraham's bosom before things were finally set to rights. It was then and there that I privately resolved never to go to heaven if there wasn't a drier route available. It occurred to me that I might be part cat, but I hadn't yet heard of reincarnation and karma, a far more likely explanation not only for my phobia, but for my "wet lungs" as well. I was supposed to "grow out of" that condition too—such, at least, was the opinion of numerous physicians to whom I was taken for diagnosis. Wrong again. I grew *into* it, and with a vengeance.

All the time I was coughing up more and more nasty, greenish-yellow sputum and running higher and higher temperatures attributed to everything from "milk fever" to "rabbit fever"—whatever that is—no farther away than St. Louis was a doctor who pioneered in lung surgery in America and who, *the very same year I was born*, had written a definitive book that takes its title, *Bronchiectasis*, from the disease it explores in exhaustive detail. He was the late Evarts A. Graham, MD, Professor Emeritus of Surgery at the Washington University School of Medicine when our paths finally crossed at Barnes Hospital in 1949. He was also the first to do research leading to discovery of a connection between smoking and lung cancer. He himself stopped smoking on the strength of his conclusions, but too late. Ironically, that was what killed him. In accordance with a prior pact with his wife, he was cremated and his ashes simply washed down the drain.

Hardly on the best-seller list, *Bronchiectasis* apparently failed to attract much attention even among physicians out in the provinces; otherwise, somebody would certainly have hailed me as a *bona fide* classic victim of that affliction—"classic" with some major differences: I wasn't dead by the age of ten as Graham said I should have been, and if, having exceeded my medically justified life span, I was mentally and/or physically retarded—as I also should have been—the impairment merely scaled me down to socially acceptable dimensions. On both counts.

Poor "Mullo"—the name that had stuck ever since my first butchered attempts at calling her "Mother." I knew whereof I spoke as I was wheeled into the operating room at Barnes the summer I was fourteen. I told Dr. Graham if he took out a rib, not to fashion from it another me, because my mother couldn't handle two of us.

Not only had she been saddled with as willful a character as the sun ever shined on, I had a weird disease nobody could cure and a chronic depression that went along with it. Two things balanced out the ledger and probably saved her sanity—and mine: first, an inordinate variety and degree of native talents that kept me fairly interested in living and, second, Anamary. Any book touching upon my mother must also include her sister for all the reasons that follow and a great many more.

The second child and first daughter of John Alison Frank and Sylvania Feroba Buchanan, Barbara Anamary was born in 1882 in Dent County, Missouri, near the town of Salem. There would be three more boys before she got her most cherished desire in 1890: a baby sister named Gracie Sylvania. Another boy came along ten years later when Vany thought her child-bearing days were over and done with. Because of her frail constitution and repeated pregnancies, a large part of the household chores fell to Anamary (whose name came from her mother's favorite novel) at a very tender age. She cooked her first meal for the family at eight, and an extant tintype of her at nine reveals a solemn little face with a maturity far beyond its years. It immediately leads one to suspect that this child never laughed or played, but that was far from true. In hardship, even as in the middle of war, children, with their incredible resilience, will find—or, more accurately, make—some time to be children. In the face of such tenacity, it renders the damage that adults inflict upon them all the more tragic.

John Frank farmed and worked in a sawmill, and the family got by, but it was not easy to feed and clothe six growing children. Vany corded and spun her own yarn and knitted stockings for her brood. Times were not much better than those described some twenty years earlier by an anonymous writer whose unfinished letter I found preserved in an ancient, crumbling Bible discovered among Mother's effects after she died. Dated November 19, 1868, and penned in that elegant, wispy hand characteristic of the day, it is addressed to "my dear friends" and goes on

> i take my pen in hand to let you know that we are all well as coman and i hope thes few lines find you all Well and doing Well heth [health?] is verry good hear in this country times is myty hard hear money is scearse hear every thing high Wheat $1 50 cts pur bus corn 50 cts crops is verry good hear in this settlement I Want to see you all mity bad.

The Franks had migrated to Missouri from North Carolina. Perhaps it was intended for someone there. Why the missive was not completed and mailed will never be known, but its pathos reaches across the years.

If things had been bad before, they became intolerable after a cataclysm that descended out of the sky late one April evening in 1893, when Mother was two years old. It had turned unseasonably hot that day, and the boys pulled off their shoes, happy to be free of that annoying winter encumbrance. In spite of the beguiling sunlight, however, low, heavy thunder rumbled in the southwest all afternoon, and towards dusk an ominous black cloud came up rapidly, accompanied by a steady flicker of lightning. Supper over, Anamary and Walter had just gone to the kitchen to do their nightly chores of washing dishes and cleaning up when their father called them back into the living quarters of the rude log cabin whose two rooms were separated by an open but roofed breezeway. He didn't like the uncanny deadness of the atmosphere and the strange roar that seemed to be getting louder. It became pitch dark as the sound took on the semblance of many deafening freight trains combined; then all hell broke loose. In the inky blackness, heavy logs began crashing about them as a tornado struck and seemed in its progress to pummel them for an eternity. Anamary recalled to me many times how it "hailed balls of fire" (ball lightning, I assume) and how she knew that Mother, at least, was still alive, for she could hear her screaming above the terrible din.

When the whirlwind passed on, John began calling out names. Miraculously, everyone answered. Vany had been sitting in a rocking chair with Gracie on her lap. The twister knocked it over so that she fell on top of the small child, protecting her, and she herself was covered with heavy quilts off a bed. Pieces of the chair were later found two miles away. In the immediate wake of the storm, the temperature plunged abruptly and it began to rain hard. The boys' feet all but freezing in the cold mud, the family made their way in the dark as best they could toward John's mother's, afraid at every step that they would find her house demolished too, and her dead.

It is impossible to sit in a place of comfort and safety and imagine what they felt in their hearts to see the twinkle of lamps in the grandmother's windows. A shoreline never looked sweeter to a shipwrecked sailor than that yellow glow did to the small band of bruised and shaken survivors. John had a cut on his forehead, and six-year-old Claud had a broken thumb—minor injuries indeed, considering what they had all crawled out from under. Some scars didn't show. A hard wind out of a clear, blue sky would send the little ones into near hysteria for ever so long afterwards. When a door banged shut one day, Neuburn, who was four, took off running down the road and had to be caught and consoled before he could be persuaded to return. It was little wonder that he had a storm cellar only three or four yards from his back door when he married and settled down.

Constructed of concrete, it projected above the ground like a half-buried crypt and made a jolly place to play when I was a kid. I preferred it over the other uncles' cellars, not so much because of its resistance to wind as its impregnability to snakes, for theirs were rude caves dug into hillsides and closed up with wooden doors. In the musty gloom of these dark recesses, serpents occasionally left their calling cards on a shelf in the form of discarded skins among the jars of canned fruits and vegetables. I was never sure how lately their former occupants had moved out. Had push come to shove, however, I would have taken a chance with the snakes over that of reaching Oz.

John Frank lost everything he had in the "cyclone" with the exception of one terrified cow that the freakish wind had deposited in the smokehouse amidst timbers from the roof. Its walls remained standing undisturbed. The rest of the stock had totally disappeared. Thoroughly disheartened, he soon moved the family to Stoddard County with what little he could scrape together. There he died eight years later, already a white-haired "old" man at fifty. Mother was twelve and her baby brother two. She would never fully recover from that bereavement, for she had been "Daddy's girl" too long to make a graceful adjustment. All the rest of her life she remembered standing on the porch the day of his funeral wondering how the sun dared to shine so brightly and the birds to sing so cheerfully.

Her father's death left Anamary with even more responsibilities, but it was not the crushing blow that yet another death imposed. Engaged to be married, she awaited the arrival of her fiancé one Saturday evening with all the giddy anticipation to which a young woman in love is entitled. He did not come. Instead, a messenger brought word that he had been killed felling a tree. It was from Mother that I heard the account when I was old enough to respect a confidence. The topic was never spoken of again in my presence. Such was the honor paid privacy in my background that, as close as we came to be, it would never have occurred to me to broach the subject with my aunt—or anyone else, for that matter. She only alluded to it obliquely a few times in reflecting upon the bitter disappointment that characterized her lot in life.

True to the man she loved, Anamary never went out with anyone again. The void created by her tragic loss and her subsequent disinclination to violate the memory of her commitment made her the logical and inevitable candidate as the one who would remain at home and become the mainstay for an ailing mother and younger siblings. The painstaking perfection with which she did everything brought upon her a more disproportionate amount of work than might otherwise have been necessary, for although she shielded her younger sister from the brunt of hard physical labor, such tasks as ironing the endless succession of their brothers' high starched collars fell to her by specific request. They knew all too well Gracie's casual, haphazard approach to matters of such moment; a man's collar, after all, said a lot about him at the turn of the last century, and they were not disposed to trust their image to so careless a guardian.

Although Anamary has been dead almost twenty years now, the patience and persistence she devoted to every task she undertook still cast a long shadow over my own predilection for summary dismissal of irksome detail. Faced with a hopelessly snarled wad of yarn that I am about to dispatch with the scissors, for instance, I am caught at the last second by a still, small voice that stays my hand.

"What would Anamary do?" it asks.

"Anamary would sit here and untangle this god-awful mess," I reply in resigned surrender, and that's what I do.

It was I, more than all the other nieces and nephews, who turned out to be the beneficiary of Anamary's self-imposed spinsterhood. She came to our house on a trial basis after Grandma died and ended up remaining there permanently. I was three and she was fifty-five, but I called her my "sister" and became very indignant when informed by outsiders that I had the kinship wrong. Her hair was still its natural rich, dark brown with a highlight of auburn, and her face was that of a woman at least twenty years younger. I didn't know what was happening at the time, but I learned later that she didn't enter menopause until well after she came to us. For her sake, maybe it was all to the good that she never got married! It is downright scary to contemplate how many children she would theoretically have been capable of bearing, even had they come at the standard two-year intervals.

As an aside, the record of parturition among my adopted relatives was held on the Brannon side of the tree onto which I was grafted: one of Dad's sisters had eighteen children, all but one of whom lived, I believe. I don't know any Roman Catholics or Orthodox Jews who can hold a candle—votive, Shabbos, or otherwise—to that. *Deo gratias!* Religious fanatics seem to forget that the adjuration to "be fruitful and multiply" was supposedly addressed to a couple who had the earth all to themselves—an earth not as yet groaning under the burden of refuse or scarred by the ravages of both human need and human greed.

To continue, however, Anamary then became my "Nurse Cummie," the beloved nanny to whom Robert Louis Stevenson dedicated his *A Child's Garden of Verses*. She was my playmate, my confidante, the buffer between me and the wrath of God; she sat up half the night at a time warming cloths over a coal-oil lamp to apply on aching ears or throbbing sinuses and walked miles helping me learn to roller-skate and ride a bike. She read whole novels to me long before I mastered that art, *Jane Eyre* standing out in my memory like a dazzling white cameo against a matrix of black. When her voice would fail from overuse, I goaded her unmercifully trying to ascertain if it was back in working condition. How I loved to sit plastered against her side on the sofa, marveling that anyone could turn those mysterious marks into the noble, sonorous words that were coming out of her mouth. What a blessing for me it never crossed her mind that I might be too young to digest the literary menu she was dishing up. She wisely read to entertain us both.

Mother and she divided the housework between them by mutual consent. Mother cooked, washed dishes and helped on washday, and Anamary did everything else. That included mowing a sizable lawn, tending a large vegetable garden in the summer, making beds, cleaning house, ironing, washing windows, clearing out eaves troughs twice a year, baking on Saturday for the hordes of relatives that always dropped in "unexpectedly" on Sundays, and carrying armloads of groceries many blocks home from the store that a woman wouldn't think of toting from a supermarket to the parking lot now.

Most remarkable of all, in the forty-five years Anamary was destined to make her home in Gracie's, I swear by all that is holy to anybody that these two never had an argument or, in my presence at least, even exchanged a cross word. When I became acquainted with my in-laws after my first marriage and learned of sisters who hadn't spoken to each other in years—and that this is scarcely a rare thing to boot—I wondered if perhaps I hadn't actually grown up on another planet. *Civilization,* in any event, meant something entirely different to me from what it meant to the rest of the world I came to know. I was also introduced at the same time to hysterical women and was utterly flabbergasted. Voices simply were not raised at our house, although my father's *dadburns* sometimes got rather loud, especially when he was running the railroads or the government from his easy chair.

I should add for the sake of posterity that "washday" meant scrubbing everything from sheets to Dad's many pairs of train-grimy overalls on a corrugated metal washboard propped in a huge galvanized tub of very hot water boiled on the kitchen stove and packed outside (or down to the basement in winter), then rinsing each item twice—once in clear water and once in a tub treated with bluing—and laboriously wringing it out by hand each time. Another receptacle of starch was provided for all the cotton items. I still remember vividly how twisted sheets snaked up the laundresses' bare arms and dangled like pythons nearly to the ground. They always stopped short somehow just before hitting the dirt. That was no mean trick, since both Mother and Anamary were only five-feet-five and very slightly built. Washday was one of my favorite times when I was a child. From the dirt moistened by water slopping out of the tubs, I made mud pies—mud pies, mud cakes, mud cookies, mud biscuits—embellishing the cakes lavishly with mud decorations and soapsuds icing. These wares were arranged on stair-step bakeries for purchase by discriminating dolls and an occasional lucky cat.

Another special time was the afternoons when I just hung around and breathed deeply (as deeply as my sick lungs would permit) while Anamary took stiff, dry clothes off the lines, sprinkled each item, rolled it into a tight ball and stashed it in a bushel basket lined with oilcloth so it would be properly moist for the next day's ironing. There is no other aroma in the world like dampened clean clothes that have dried in the open air—unless it's the similar scent of approaching rain on parched, warm earth.

I remember well the first permanent-press garment I ever saw. It was a blouse belonging to a girl from Oregon who lived down the hall from me in the dorm at Washington University. I was utterly amazed and declared that this marvelous fabric would revolutionize the world. It would free women forever from the tyranny of the ironing board. What happened? One-hundred percent cotton came back with a vengeance just when I had three sons and a husband who all wore shirts.

Mother somehow found time to make our clothes and Anamary to crochet a wide assortment of items from doilies to baby layettes. We used to say she crocheted "by ear," since she could duplicate anything by merely looking at it.

The dresses they wore to do the morning's work each day were pulled off after lunch and replaced with clean ones. They rested in the afternoon, although their hands were seldom idle then. Hats were a must, whether they went to church or merely to the grocery store, for it was the Nineteenth Century that had shaped their personal habits. Just as Anamary continued to call my bicycle a "wheel" and expressed a need to "go out" rather than "go to the bathroom," till this very day I refer to refrigerators as "ice boxes" and will continue to do so as long as I live. Some conditioning simply won't bend to changing times. The iceman making his rounds door to door with his huge black tongs and fifty-pound blocks of dripping crystal are still as real to me as yesterday's sunset. His arrival was an event.

I don't intend to pose as a sentimentalist, advocating a return to those difficult days from which we've indeed come a long way, baby. What is instructive about them is the dignity that women like Mother and Anamary lent to hard physical labor. They didn't complain about it, and they bore themselves like gentlewomen, never confusing duty with drudgery or associating human worth with the amount and quality of leisure available. Their example is still pertinent.

CHAPTER THREE

For some reason, my legal adoption was postponed until I was three. Before it could be effected, notice had to be publicized a given number of times to provide my actual mother an opportunity to return and claim me. Even though the announcement appeared in a legal rag not commonly accessible to, much less read by, the public at large, every knock on the door during that waiting period sounded like Gabriel's trumpet. Doomsday lurked just beyond that wooden panel. But it always turned out to be a neighbor or a tramp wanting a handout or somebody selling brushes or Watkins products. No one showed up to snatch me away, so the court decreed I could continue to be who I had already become, and I was issued a new birth certificate that put the matter to rest once and for all.

No sooner was that settled than another threat followed close on the heels of its predecessor. Dad was discovered to have "an old Jane" at the other end of his run. "There's always something to take the joy out of life," Mother used to say. Back to court she went, and I was told that my father wouldn't be living with us anymore. Whether I had already picked up on the fact that I was ensconced in a matriarchy or really was an insufferable egotist is uncertain. My response to the news, at any rate, was a shrug of the shoulders and this unconcerned retort: "That's okay. You've still got me."

But it wasn't quite "okay." Mother was confronted with the prospect of having to provide a living for us, and—although she had briefly taught school years before—she had grave doubts about being able to enter the job market, such as it was in 1938, at her age and still with delicate health. She therefore reconsidered, and before the estrangement became permanent and litigated, she agreed to a reconciliation—of sorts. It left her pretty much at the helm, as far as I could ever determine, and what it probably did for Dad's sex life is mercifully left to the imagination. The insult to Mother's pride surfaced in myriad subtle ways. I grew up with the distinct impression that the worst thing a woman can do is teach school and the second worst is to marry. Having done both more than once, I can't say she was altogether wrong.

A much more serious side effect of her decision was the occasional reminder that it was for my sake that Mother bore the cross of a marriage gone sour. It was not a responsibility I wanted or appreciated, and as a result, I determined never to sacrifice any children I might have on the altar of financial security. The pendulum went its ineluctable way, and now my boys are just as determined never to put their offspring through the wringer of divorce. *C'est la vie.*

It was small wonder that Anamary became my Rock of Gibraltar. While Mother was on an emotional roller coaster, Anamary was *there*, unchanged and unchanging. There to hold me tightly when nightmares left me paralyzed with fear; there to sob in her arms after my switchings for disobedience or recalcitrance; there to encourage me when I wanted to give up; there, in short, to love me quietly and nonpossessively and patiently and loyally.

Her attachment was reciprocated in full measure, but that did not stop me from venting my childish spleen on her at times. Even during those sudden squalls that were most likely to blow up when she combed my hair—"You're pulling on purpose!" was a familiar refrain—I never drifted far from that anchor of a steady and tacit devotion. On the occasion of one such row, Mother, who was busy tending the burning coal in our living-room heater, pulled the hot poker out of the firebox and said to me in mock support of my unjust accusations, "Maybe I ought to just hit her with this poker!" Thinking she was serious, I sprang from Anamary's lap and threw out my arm to ward off what I thought was an imminent blow before either woman could prevent me from getting a bad burn.

Only four at the time, I wouldn't have hesitated to go through fire itself to protect my idol.

If Mother ever resented the role her sister played in my upbringing, she never showed it. Perhaps she understood the need for a balance, and since the unpleasant task of meting out discipline fell entirely to her, she was probably as thankful as I was that I had a psychological refuge in which to lick my wounds. Both of these dear women later provided the same invaluable refuge for each of my sons in turn when I was left with the same unpleasant task. The closest my father ever came to wielding his authority was to threaten to tell Mother if I did something I wasn't supposed to do.

Mother was not a sadist by any stretch of the imagination, nor did her methods of discipline constitute "child abuse." They broke no bones nor left any scars. She simply believed—as most sane people do—that children running amok do more violence to domestic tranquility than the normal human adult can bear. Judging from the number of youngsters I know of now who dominate and terrorize their parents and drive teetotalers to drink, the mounting incidence of real child abuse comes as no surprise. The parent who does not set and enforce reasonable—emphasis on *reasonable*—limits will break at some point of intolerance, and all too often it's at an extreme of frustration where restraint is emotionally almost impossible. Little angels are not born, they're made, and the young woman who wants babies because they're cute and cuddly would be well advised never to give up playing with dolls rather than become pregnant. And nobody—absolutely nobody—should ever have a child who has not previously had a pet that poops in the floor and destroys everything of value within reach. That is the proper test run for parenthood. If the pet lives, its owner *may* be capable of parenting.

Those who are unable to distinguish between enlightened discipline and child abuse should read Dorothy L. Sayers' delightful story "Talboys" written in 1942 and first published in a collection of her short who-done-its entitled *Lord Peter*, so named for her fictional British peer-cum-sleuth, Lord Peter Wimsey. The villain of the piece is a Miss Quirk, who had "studied the subject" of child psychology (God help us!) and is therefore a self-proclaimed expert on same. For all her high-blown criticism of Lord Peter's exercise of parental authority, she ends up paddling a young Wimsey for all she's worth on account of something he didn't even do. (It was actually the redoubtable peer of the realm himself who put the live snake in her bed.)

The Miss Quirks of the world who sowed the seeds of permissiveness (the rotten fruits of which we are now trying to digest with some difficulty) apparently forgot that discipline is not only crucial to sanity, but to survival as well—laying the matter of character-building aside. It is found among all mammals as far as I'm aware; otherwise, most species we know would have disappeared from the earth long, long ago without human assistance. Young things that don't heed their mamas' warnings generally get eaten or break their ignorant little necks.

I will never forget something I was privileged to witness once. We had a cat whose kittens were just at that exploratory age toddlers go through. My folks and I were all sitting in the back yard watching them tumble around and play when the most aggressive of them started to climb a tree. His mother made a strange, throaty sound, and he turned away. But again he ventured back. Again she communicated the same warning. This time he paid her no mind and proceeded up the tree trunk.

She leaped up from where she had been lying in watchful repose, shinned up the tree after him, wrapped one front paw around his back legs and jerked him down to the ground, where she gave him such a box on the ears that he went rolling away in a little fur ball. A similar account is given about the lioness Elsa of *Born Free* and *Living Free*. She was determined that her cubs should not cross a certain river infested with crocodiles. When one persisted in his disobedient efforts to do so, she swam to him, grabbed him by the neck and held his head under the water until he was more than willing to scramble for the bank and stay put.

Cats, big and little, are very intelligent creatures, of course, as well as courageous. The puss of the tree-climbing episode was so protective of her babies that she actually chased stray dogs out of the yard. Sometimes we would be in the house and see a white blur streak by a window.

"White Kitty must be after a dog," someone would say and go look. There she'd be at the heels of a much larger—and retreating—canine. I always figured as a mother myself that I could do a lot worse than live up to her standards of maternity.

Even birds discipline their young. I was waiting for a bus one time near a sapling that contained a nest of young cardinals. The parents took turns coming and going with insect delicacies, one of them always staying at the site. Doddering small heads, seventy-percent beak, could be seen waving about. Then one adventurous youngster poked his over the rim of the nest for a look-see down below. Mama pecked him smartly on the noggin, and he did not emerge again as long as I stood there watching.

Two relevant examples of what I'm driving at in terms of survival come instantly to mind. We lived in a house that was considerably below street level when I was a child. On the front and one side, allowance for the discrepancy was made by a high, concrete retaining wall topped by a picket fence. I had a neighbor a year or so older than I whose company I thought I preferred above anyone else's and whose lead I believed I should be permitted to follow. She was fond of displaying her derring-do by walking the narrow ledge of the wall inside the pickets, a feat denied me by my mother, who obviously knew nothing about fun and was, *ipso facto*, unfair.

One day Bette was showing off her stuff when she decided to jump down from the wall to the yard below. I held my breath in worshipful admiration. Unfortunately, as she launched herself into the air, the hem of her dress caught on a picket, impeding her takeoff. She therefore slid straight down the wall, her bare back leaving bits of flesh on the cement all the way to the ground. My recollection is that she screamed for the rest of the afternoon. If there's anyone living still who was part of the neighborhood at the time, he or she may have a slightly different memory. It could have been until the next morning. Typical of those Puritans who enjoy seeing other people suffer for what they themselves would have liked to do, I thought to myself that she jolly well deserved just what she got. And I secretly didn't think quite so ill of my mother's sense of justice—for a while.

A more tragic case was that of two children I knew about my age who had been told, as I was, not to play in ponds, which, in Missouri, usually look like liquid mud or big basins of *café au lait*. I never had any trouble respecting injunctions against venturing in, since ponds hold water. If that hadn't been enough of a deterrent to disobedience, another one would have sufficed: they also hold snakes that come to eat frogs. And little girls. The younger sibling, a girl, apparently waded in over her head, and her brother tried to save her. They both drowned.

"Honor thy father and thy mother," says the Commandment, "*so that thy days may be long upon the earth.*" Better believe. Of course, the Author of that gem had more than the natural benefits of obedience in mind. Provision is made in Mosaic Law for parents to take obstinate children before a convocation of Elders empowered with the authority to have them stoned to death. Strange that one so seldom hears a sermon on that text (*Deuteronomy* 21:18-21). I myself delivered one once en route home in the car with my husband and three sons. The latter were occupying the back seat together, but not amiably. I had issued several warnings that fell on deaf ears. As we approached a tack shop, I instructed my husband to pull over. When he did, I got out and went inside, leaving behind some seriously curious people.

On returning to the car with my purchase—a lethal looking riding crop—I announced that it *would* be quiet in the back seat the rest of the way home. It was.

This is perhaps an appropriate place to quote an old doggerel I grew up on:

> Don't slap baby in the face.
> Nature provided a better place.

Unfortunately, nobody commanded parents to honor their children or even to display a generous measure of common sense in exacting honor for themselves. Even Mother, in all her wisdom, sometimes did very strange things. The one that sticks like a cocklebur to the fuzzy nap of my memory caused a great deal of confusion in my singularly literal mind that wasn't really resolved for years. It came about because she had what she was pleased to think of as a sense of humor, a characteristic often lacking both sense *and* humor!

A man passed our house four times on weekdays going to and from his work as a shoe salesman. We sometimes bought shoes from him and always exchanged casual greetings when he went by, but as far as I know, he remained nameless. One afternoon I was helping my father wash the car by manning the hose while he applied a soapy rag. It was a weighty responsibility, and I was appropriately impressed with my capacity to fill it. I was standing on the parkway between the sidewalk and the street, and Mother was looking on from the back-porch swing. Along came the ill-fated shoe salesman, returning to the store from lunch. He was dressed in suit and tie, and his shoes were polished.

Just as he drew up even with me, smiling his respects to the family, Mother—for reasons probably not known even to God—said, "Turn the hose on him, June!"

Incredulous at the directive but true to my conditioning, I did precisely that. I turned the hose on him. Not just a little bit, but head on and full force. Right then I got a crash course in jurisprudence, learning that "You *told* me to!" doesn't quite cut it, a lesson Nazi war criminals also discovered after the fact. Among other immediate repercussions, I was relieved of all further contact with the garden hose, and, in rather the same mode as the black tomcat and for the same reasons, the unlucky gentleman favored the other side of the street for his comings and goings from then on.

Averse to resorting to a hickory every time I got out of line, Mother displayed a genius for creating alternatives. I had a penchant for fighting, even as a two-year-old. Reliable reports have it that I belted her across the face at that age on being told to do something I didn't choose to do. We were on Grandma's porch, and Mother immediately clapped her hand to her cheek and went inside, where she smeared red food coloring on the assaulted area. She returned to the porch faking severe pain and allowed her hand to reveal just enough "blood" to wring tears from a marble statue. I never struck her again.

Her clever response didn't prevent me from taking my peers to the dirt on occasion, especially after I started to school and encountered the usual smattering of bullies. (Yes, Virginia. We had bullies in 1942—before TV and egomania.) The problem became sufficiently serious that a note from the good Mother Perpetua, a dear old Ursuline nun, summoned Mother to school for a conference: how could they discourage the fisticuffs and also preserve my proclivity for championing the cause of hectored underdogs? It was a knotty dilemma that wise heads of state have failed to solve for millennia. I don't recall, since I wasn't in on the discussion, what they came up with. Perhaps Nature intervened with the perfect answer. The bullies were all boys and soon outgrew me. It doesn't take many brains to avoid physical combat when the odds are clearly against winning.

I continued to be known as "the little mother of the playground," though, and on being asked one afternoon on arriving home how things had gone that day, I sighed as if carrying the world on my shoulders and replied, "I just wish God hadn't made little Billie Brickle." I was painfully aware of my limitations in respect to protecting him adequately. There have been many times over the years when I could profitably have called that lesson to mind and didn't.

Knowing better than ever to sass my mother back, I sometimes expended my remarkable temper on inanimate things such as staircases. On one of these occasions, I was made to stomp up and down them with the fury of a Rumpelstiltskin until the soles of my feet smarted—even through my shoes—and I was more than happy to tread with ladylike decorum. She also pursued me through the house from time to time fanning me furiously with a magazine to "cool" me off. Once she consulted Doctor Annie after I had thrown a fit that included kicking like a mule and banging my head on the floor. She was advised that if it ever happened again, she should just dash a bucket of cold water in my face. I haven't the least doubt that would have worked, but it never became necessary. I must have figured out that there were more desirable ways to assert myself in the conduct of psychological warfare than to endanger my gray matter.

Mother's ingenuity extended to the invention of a crown somewhere in the Great Beyond from which one or more constituent stars fell every time I was bad, depending upon the nature of the offense. These losses really worried me, and I was careful to reverse them between relapses. To her enduring credit, I was never chastised in anger and very rarely without some preliminary opportunity to choose a more agreeable disposition of the conflict at hand. As I grew older, I was sufficiently aware of the ground rules that most of the time I knew when I had it coming. The problem, of course, was that I didn't always agree with the ground rules, and I was not consulted when it came to drawing them up. When my options were exhausted respecting their implementation, Mother could—and did—make feathers fly all over the place without ruffling a single one of her own. It was a gift—one that I came to envy her when I was reduced to near apoplexy by my own youngsters years later.

Here, more than anywhere else, the discontinuity of DNA was baldly evident. When I tried to be Mother, I usually failed miserably. It should be mentioned, however, that she might have failed miserably at being herself given three boys instead of one girl! I may have taken crayons to the bedstead, but I never took a razor blade to newly upholstered velvet settees nor built fires under the house. Interestingly enough, her reaction to the former mischief was to sew up the gash with needle and thread and to plead for mercy on the miscreant's behalf. Perhaps she had learned something she never shared with me in the interim following the nipple incident.

Much of the time, Mother was a benevolent dictator; otherwise, my ambivalence towards her could not have been so acute. This is a natural phenomenon, of course, epitomizing the classic idea of the "mother venerated"—that is, loved and hated during childhood—who finds expression in the mythical Lilith, legendary first wife of Adam. I fondly recall putting Mother's featherbed on the floor once (albeit only once!) so a young friend and I could have a wrestling match on it. I must also admit that I was prone to run laps through the house with my dog Wiggles in hot pursuit, his toenails skidding on slick linoleums and propelling him headlong into any piece of furniture (or human being) in harm's way. I was careful to keep such particulars of my history as these to myself when drawing upon my own childhood for an exemplary model from which my children would derive much-needed instruction. Confession is not always good for other people's souls.

Only twice did I think Mother truly unjust, and the grudges remained on my heart like blackberry stains on a white pinafore. I made it a point to clear up one of them after we both knew her death was imminent. I asked her one day when we were kind of cleaning our respective slates why she came after me the time I was sitting on the blanket with Bette petting her new puppy. I was four or five. There I was in seventh heaven, and there came Mother with Old Reliable, the Ever-Ready Yardstick. I couldn't imagine what infraction of the law I was committing, so I quickly put the dog down, just in case. She still advanced on me, yardstick poised. Too proud to ask before or after she applied it, I went through the next forty-four years, believe it or not, wondering what I had done. She told me: I had broken the rule about not playing on the parkway close to the street. Ah so!

The other instance was a bit stickier. I knew what the punishment was for, but I was powerless to convince her of my innocence. We were having one of those "head-start" sessions that used to be carried out at home. Mine enabled me to read and write (in very legible script) before ever starting to school and promoted me from the first to the third grade when I did go.

The particular lesson in question was the names of the days of the week. For some reason, I had a mental block about Monday (which happens to be the weekday on which I was born). Every other day rolled right off the tip of my tongue, but when Monday got there, it dug in its heels like a novice on a high diving board. Mother, who was a fanatic when it came to stubborn children, quite honestly believed I was deliberately refusing to cooperate. When all other persuasions failed to elicit the right response, she marched outside to one of our always handy trees for a motivating factor. Old Reliable had been mysteriously broken.

While she was gone, Anamary kept repeating over and over, "Say Monday! Say Monday!" I had every intention of saying "Monday" when Mother came back. But did I? Absolutely not. I went blank again, like the bank's computers every time you desperately need to know your balance. I got the motivating factor and still vividly recall sitting on Anamary's lap, sobbing into her bosom, aware that she, at least, knew I was not just being contrary. Children do forget, and stress does short out the brain—two things a parent needs to remember at all times.

I've often thought how difficult it must have been for Anamary to remain neutral, never butting in, never expressing her displeasure at the way things were done or not done. I haven't always managed to do that with my grandchildren. She had her own inimitable way of bending me to her will, of course. It largely consisted of an immensely original repertory of Didactic Gems for All Occasions. A beautiful case in point follows.

We were parked at the railway station during World War II watching the troop trains go by—a pastime I only vaguely understood had something to do with my father's having been in the army during the previous Big One. I don't know what solace our being there afforded those forlorn-looking young men. It certainly afforded my dad none, for he always went home weeping silently.

Anyway, the local Quasimodo happened to hobble by on badly clubbed feet—a spectacle bound to arouse my curiosity.

Anamary quickly explained that he got that way by wearing his mother's high-heeled shoes when he was a lad of precisely my age. Information like this gave me the reputation among my small friends of being something of a doomsayer, since I was not one to keep good advice to myself. It did not deter them from clomping around in *their* mothers' high heels, though, and much to my consternation, none of them got clubbed feet—or even sprained an ankle.

CHAPTER FOUR

I've read a good many autobiographies in recent years, mostly bitter things by women who seem to have grown up in zoos. Not one of them but what has a lurid account of Discovering That Parents Have Sex (or Neighbors or Neighbors and Parents). I missed out on all that good stuff, since my father—despite his fall from grace (no pun intended)—was the quintessence of Victorian modesty around the house. Sitting on the front porch one Fourth of July evening after an ample supper, he forgot he had loosened his belt and jumped up to look at somebody's Roman candle—and almost died of embarrassment when the inevitable happened. There would scarcely have been more scrambling and "Dad-burning!" if his trousers had been on fire.

I was somewhere around three when Mother first attempted to enlighten me regarding the difference between girls and boys. She had only begun her spiel when I interrupted her with a very blasé "Oh, I know. I don't have any ding-dong like that on *me*!" The inflection clearly indicated an emphatic "Thank God!" She was so taken aback by my rather adroit depiction of anatomy that she never delved into the source of my education, and *ding-dong* became the family euphemism for *penis* ever after. Conveniently, I might add, for in my background bulls were called *papa cows* and some things were just not mentioned.

I taught a course called "Women in Society" at Southeast Missouri State University many years later and read in the textbook anthology for the first time Sigmund Freud's "The Psychical Consequences of the Anatomical Distinction Between the Sexes"—and laughed myself sick. A little girl, he opines, sees a penis for the first time, notes that she is without one and immediately desires to own that singular appendage. She feels "mutilated" without it. Now, wasn't that astute of the gentleman! Not only did I fail to consider myself deprived, I exulted in my own streamlined contours.

On becoming an adult, my encounters with the male genitals added nothing to my early assessment of them. The unerected penis, to my mind, has to be the most pitiful and vulnerable organ conceivable. I could never quite understand how men ride horseback comfortably, though I confess that I never cared enough to inquire. The penis becomes only slightly less pitiful erected and even more vulnerable. It further becomes—let's be honest now—just a little bit funny. It also has the misfortune of being almost totally at the mercy of every emotion in the book, either collapsing like a punctured balloon at the very moment a bit of starch would do nicely or standing at attention when the brain is shouting "At ease!" Mark Twain knew why women have the edge. Anyone confused about that should check out his *Letters From the Earth* sometime!

Orthodox male Jews can thank God they're not women every morning until hell freezes over and Moshiach turns Crown Heights (New York headquarters of Lubavitch Chassidism) into the New Jerusalem, but I'll keep my gender, thank you just the same. Certain Jewish Kabbalists are even on record as proclaiming that wicked males are punished by being females in their next incarnation. The growing number of gay men would seem to suggest just the opposite! But who's to say. The growing number of feminists out to prove that women are merely men in disguise might be taken to support the contention. What I can proclaim with some confidence is that the only advantage men have to my knowledge—genitally speaking—is the enviable one of not needing to bare their entire backsides when doing, as Bill Cosby puts it, "God's work"—God's "number-one work," at least—in cold weather. I date back to the rural outdoor privy, the bane of my young existence and the source of occasional accidents as well as much constipation.

This is not to say that I don't like men or wish to disparage manhood. Quite the contrary. I've loved my share of them—and probably then some. Besides, what's a mother of sons to do?

But there is no room for a "better half" in my concept of the scheme of things. The fellow who considers himself something special just because of a physical characteristic common to all male animals had better give me a very wide berth, and the husband who imagines he can make reparation for any manner and amount of emotional damage he has inflicted merely by waving that clapper in my face is well advised to ring someone else's bell with it—permanently. If you want to meet a woman who really hates men, you have only as far to go as the nearest whorehouse.

Contrary to Freud's prognosis, if I ever developed a "wound to my narcissism" in consequence of my deprivation, I was never aware of it, nor did I ever feel inferior to men (not since I've lived with indoor plumbing). At no time in my upbringing was it ever suggested that my gender was a handicap or that my future role was cut out for me. The sky was the limit (with the two notable exceptions already mentioned in passing). I was exempted from any kind of housework (thanks to Anamary), and I didn't learn to cook from my mother. It was reasoned that childhood should not entail responsibilities that would come soon enough in the regular course of events. There was a feeble and short-lived attempt to teach me to sew, and for a brief time I busied myself with learning to embroider. My enthusiasm for the craft was cured when Mother made me finish a set of seven dish towels I had insisted must be mine if I was to live a minute longer. Each displayed the name of a different day and pictured a kitten engaged in whatever activity was traditionally appropriate to it: washing, ironing, mending, shopping, baking, etc. By the time I got through, I wanted to wring its industrious yellow neck.

It was never even hinted to me in my formative years that my being a girl stood between me and anything I was intelligent enough and dogged enough to accomplish. The goal towards which I was nudged was to achieve that status which would render me totally independent—not beholding to any man *or* woman. I missed it by the indeterminate country mile, but not before vacillating among any number of early ambitions. At one time I planned quite seriously to become an astronomer. If I had known about paleontology then, that would have topped the list. In their turn, the convent, medicine, art, music, the theater and the foreign missions caught my fancy.

I played with dolls and decked my long-suffering cats out in their finery, but so did I play with trucks and airplanes and pretend to be a bank teller, a game warden, and a railroad dispatcher. I also dressed up like the Virgin Mother occasionally and assumed the pious attitude of a statue on the piano bench, but somewhere along the line I learned that most of us can't have it both ways.

Another of my ambitions was to go about the world releasing animals from zoos. I haven't altogether abandoned that one. I like to knit now, but I also like to pound nails into wood, and I suspect there are more of us around than rabid feminists of a few years back would like to admit. My reaction to a live debate I attended once between Schaffley and Smeal was "a plague on both your houses."

Reality is somewhere in between, and those of us who live it day in and day out had better stand up and be counted. The point is not to aspire to motherhood or corporate management or bulldozer operation as the end-all and be-all of female accomplishment, but rather to strive towards being content with who we are, with or without a ding-dong.

Excellence has, for many years, managed to assert itself in the presence of sufficient will and a cooperative Lady Luck, regardless of the gender in which it found expression, but excellence is no longer the issue. In their frenetic rush to prove something that was already obvious, strident feminists overshot their mark and inflicted upon society a glut of mediocre female employees and lousy mothers who did justice to neither their jobs nor their families when they might have functioned admirably in one role alone. As it is, their entrance into the marketplace has merely expanded and redefined the lowest common denominator of competence.

As already noted, a female doctor delivered me in 1935—but one whose workplace was also her home, and if her male peers regarded her askance, the fact still remains that she was not denied academic or legal access to their ranks. The first preacher I knew well was a woman, and I was married the first time around in 1956 by a female magistrate judge in that lady's living room, having first carefully picked my way through a clutter of toys on her porch. When I myself entered law school at the University of Arizona in 1957, I was admittedly the solitary woman in my class, but only because women were not clamoring to get in—probably because most other females at the time had more sense than I did. To my surprise, I found the study of law to be an insufferable bore designed for methodical, plodding minds not given to quickness and restive flights of creative fantasy (although the devious circumlocutions picked up there for side-stepping the truth just might come under the rubric of creativity).

I stuck it out only a year, not because I was the object of discrimination, but because I couldn't stay awake in Contracts and quoted Shakespeare rather than Black on Torts exams. The former seemed infinitely more relevant to justice. I also recall stating on an Equity final that if such a person as the hypothetical client came to me whining that his neighbor's wall was eight inches over the property line, I'd tell him to go straight to hell.

Three-fourths of the women lawyers I personally observed in operation during a stint I served many years later as a court recorder represented insurance companies against injured workers—not exactly a high calling or one that requires any but the most meager of talents save that for blistering sarcasm. Their careers could hardly be hailed as a moral victory over anything. A physician I came to know well during this period declared under oath that the attorneys for one very large workers' compensation carrier were a disgrace to their profession and that its claims adjusters, women all, were a disgrace to the human race. Our eventual friendship stemmed from a letter I wrote to him commending his perception and the courage it took to defend it in court. He was subsequently hounded out of his practice and denied a license. Any but the hopelessly naïve knows that freedom of speech, even in this bastion of so-called democracy, is largely a matter of whose ears are burning and where the money is concentrated.

But let's get back to the question of female identity: the impression younger women have about what it was like before their time puzzles me a good deal. Men have never made any secret, it seems to me, of their recognition and even fear of the power women hold over them. From Lysistrata to Lady Macbeth to Aunt Polly and the Widow Douglas, the message has been loud and clear.

What passes for the soul of a nation is not reflected in how and where it worships, but in how and by whom it is entertained—what, in short, it is willing to acknowledge as its face in the mirror of that art form most accessible to the greatest number of its citizens. Witness our current hideous TV image if you doubt that. During the Thirties and Forties, radio provided the most universally available entertainment, and it yielded up a composite picture of a pretty formidable woman. Consider the titles of the afternoon soaps: *Ma Perkins* (Oxydol's Own), *Portia Faces Life, Young Widow Brown, Mary Nobel:Backstage Wife, Abbie's Irish Rose* and my favorite as a pre-school addict, *Stella Dallas*, the chronicle of a brave widow who spent most of her time running her son-in-law's life, as I recollect. I would remind those born after 1935 that there was a deadly war going on; hence the emphasis on widowhood.

The evening-hour comedies were also dominated by strong (if sometimes wacky) women: Molly Magee, Jane Ace, Beulah, Baby Snooks, Mary Livingston, Gracie Allen. The serious saga of *One Man's Family* was the single bow to respect due a patriarch.

Comic strips of the day also caricatured family life in which women were smart and men easily duped or downright hen-pecked. The heroes like Captain Easy and Red Ryder were all bachelors and determined to stay that way. There were a few glamorous career women as well. I especially remember Brenda Starr, a newspaper reporter with the enviable capacity for becoming invisible when she so desired. (And politicians think they have a hard time now eluding the press!)

I saw Martha Hoople's stout arm and its rolling-pin extension as a variation on the theme of Mother's frail one and understood perfectly well in each instance who was best endowed by the Creator to rule the roost. It never once crossed my mind that their mental prowess might stop at the front gate. By a natural process of extrapolation, I just assumed that they could excel at anything in the way of human endeavor that required brains rather than brawn, though Martha was well blessed with that too.

Since a flashlight has none of the attributes of a garden hose, no one needed to tell me why my mother rather than I was always called upon to hold it while Dad engaged in the myriad repair projects which occupied much of his "leisure" time. Without benefit of her keen judgment and instant perception, many of the things he took apart to fix would never have been put back together again. These included everything from the family auto to the kitchen sink. Years afterwards when I advised my husband to leave the car parked at the road instead of attempting to back into the snow-packed driveway and he ignored me to the end that he not only got stuck but plowed up half the front yard in the process, I didn't even bother to gloat. It was merely history as I knew it repeating itself with monotonous regularity. I watched from the kitchen window as the car spun about, digging deeper and deeper in its search for a bit of purchase on some terra firma. Its defeated driver finally got out, saw me looking on, and threw a snowball at the window so hard that he broke it.

So pervasive was the historical concept of the domineering female that the inevitable backlash stands as a unique and—when all the evidence is in—probably tragic monument to idiocy. "Mom" became a dirty word, vis-à-vis Philip Wylie, whose message was largely misunderstood and misapplied. Its negative connotation was not embraced exclusively by the relatively few who were truly victimized by isolated instances of actual maternal tyranny that bore no resemblance to real mothering, but by succeeding generations of otherwise psychologically healthy people. Women caught hell both coming and going. They were the monsters who turned out the spineless men who, by default, later turned wives into monsters. Psychologists jumped on the bandwagon, and the crusade was official.

"Mom" was to blame for everything from war to labor strife, gangsterism to homosexuality. Jung's protégé M. Esther Harding reached back into Egyptian mythology and came up with the archetypal mother/son relationship that told the whole sordid story. Never mind that Abe Lincoln had said with forthright humility, "All that I am or ever hope to be I owe to my angel mother." Mom got crucified.

But women, alas, have the unique capacity for bearing children, so a resurrection was inevitable—nay, mandatory. The New and Improved Mom was transfigured without her old vestments of hearth and home, however. After all, she had merely wreaked havoc there, hadn't she? Somebody conveniently decided that it's not the quantity of time spent with small fry that counts, but the quality, and the babysitter became a national institution. Nobody bothered to inquire if she might be yet another kind of monster.

Mom began making money instead of cookies, progress instead of love. It wasn't very rewarding, after all, to have her superior brainpower known only to her immediate family. It had to be held up for the admiration of a much wider audience, even if she didn't really enjoy the new role she was assigned on stage. Her economic emancipation stripped Pop of the one service he had formerly provided as sole breadwinner, and he became expendable. Ergo, divorce rates shot up accordingly. They were helped along back then, of course, by the vast number of marriages consummated just hours, if not minutes, before the troop trains pulled out. Johnny often came marching home to a complete stranger who, it was suddenly discovered, bore no resemblance to the girl he left behind him.

Those women stranded in the backwash of the revolution were soon made to feel apologetic for "just being housewives," but our marvelous language eventually came to their rescue and converted them to "domestic engineers" just as it converted janitors to the much more elevated status of "building superintendents."

Like Cassandra, I saw the culmination of all this coming back in the Seventies and sent out my predictions (which have come true) to sundry magazines in the form of articles with titles like "Thirty-nine and Holding (A Few Grudges)." Editors were not interested in them, so I eventually gave up and saved my stamps for letters to God and Santa Claus, who at least never send out rejection slips. The burden of my message was "It just ain't possible, ladies. The gal who brings home the bacon still has to fry it, and she's gonna be so tired she'll probably let it burn." I didn't mention that she might not even be able to stand up, a contingency all too real.

For almost a decade, I free-lanced as a proofreader of transcriptions made from recordings of workers' compensation hearings in the State of Oregon, some of which I had taped myself. The frequency and severity of accidents befalling women in the workplace were appalling, and their stress claims outnumbered those of men ten to one. Typically, they couldn't get along with some other female employee, the workload was too heavy for their limited strength, or the boss was a dirty SOB.

It's one thing for a woman to pit her wits against a man's on the job, usually enjoying the more or less civilized protocol that demands a certain mutual *show* of respect between the sexes (former senator Bob Packwood notwithstanding), but it's quite another for her to abide subtle competition from other women whose private intimations of superiority run afoul of her own. One of the advantages women hold over men is that the latter rarely understand them. But women understand other women and are thus doomed to distrust all but a precious few proven harmless in pursuit of a common cause or by the rigors of earnest friendship. Like it or not, that's the nature of the beast, and it's apt to remain so.

The proceedings of state workers' compensation hearings are a matter of public record and therefore accessible to serious researchers or the merely curious. Someone ought to publish a book totally composed of the tearjerkers I had to read, day after day. About all a woman proves by pulling lumber on a greenchain is that when she destroys her back so doing, insurance companies would rather pay medical "experts" a thousand dollars a day to testify that the problem stems from arthritis, which she had all along, than give her any compensation.

This is so lucrative a source of easy income that many doctors make a career of being "independent medical examiners" at the beck and call of well-heeled carriers, limiting their hands-on practice of medicine to a minimum or eliminating it altogether. In conjunction with their "specialty," they sometimes conduct research that invariably bolsters the diagnoses an insurer likes to hear, violating tried and true principles of scientific method so flagrantly as to commit travesties not only upon justice, but also upon academic integrity.

The woman *or* man who punches a time clock is not free. As monotonous as some may believe housekeeping to be, it's a holiday compared to the assembly line, and as overbearing as some husbands are, they're generally not breathing down a wife's neck eight hours straight, nit-picking and threatening to kick her out in the street if her dishes aren't washed by 12:35 on the dot. The mother who stays home, knows where her kids are and what they're doing, can pace herself. She can sit down whenever she wants, lie down whenever she wants, watch TV or listen to the radio while she works or doesn't work, be as creative as she chooses and control the aesthetic quality of her environment to whatever degree her ingenuity and budget permit. She can even—guess what!—*read*! Name one "gainful employment" that allows that kind of latitude.

One of the most alarming statistics that came out of an investigation conducted by a Task Force on Drugs mandated by the Salem, Oregon, School District some years back (I was privileged to serve on it) was the vast number of students who either had no one at home after school dismissed to know or care what they did or who actually no longer lived at home but with a friend or older sibling. This often resulted from violent conflicts with a stepparent or live-in boyfriend. American women have a lot to answer for, and the reckoning is upon us.

The economic rationale for a mother's working is sometimes valid—and unfortunately becoming more so—but when this snowball first started down the incline, it was largely a myth tailored to self-centered and grossly misguided aspirations for "fulfillment" with no accurate understanding of what that really entails. Equating it with dreams of financial stability is disastrous, since people with more to spend do just that: they spend more. That is the fly in the proposed ointment of personal investments as opposed to government regulated Social Security. Financial "security," like Kipling's Kangaroo of the *Just So Stories*, remains far out in front. We Yellow Dog Dingoes always trail behind, "never getting nearer, never getting farther." How ironic that now—when the cost of living and the expense of medical care have gone way off and left the average income—*now* women are finally waking up to their physical and emotional limitations!

The change slowly began here and there almost a decade ago. "Mommy track taking U-turn," announced a headline in a July 8, 1991, issue of the now defunct *Pittsburgh Press*: "Careers put on shelf for some." Well, hallelujah! It's coming none too soon. I believe that it is up to women to seize the initiative in making the world a safe place, not for democracy or any other given *ism*, but for human existence, period. To do that they must begin again in the sphere where their influence has always been, both by necessity and opportunity, potentially greatest—in the home—so that once more we can say with the conviction of a Dorothy stranded in Oz, there's no place like it.

That is not to imply that they cannot and should not make valuable contributions on a broader scale in the absence of conflicting interests so long as they remember that it is at a mother's knee that the basic building blocks of civilized behavior must be laid, where self-discipline and consideration for the rights and feelings of others must be instilled, where the natural sociopathy with which we all come into the world is gently and gradually transformed into generous accommodation to the real structure of the universe and even to willing sacrifice on behalf of the common good.

We get such values there or not at all, for they must grow up with us rather than being imposed cosmetically after the fact. Such belated surface facades wash off in the first cold rain of personal defeat.

I will be eternally grateful that my mother did without many things, the lack of which branded us socially, and that she stayed home to wield her influence on a child who needed it badly. She skimped and saved, and I attended one of the best universities in the Midwest, winding up with four degrees from three schools before I finally called it quits. I doubt that my boys will ever go on record as being grateful to me for my extensive education, too much of which was gleaned by wearing out my eyes and rear end on useless research in myriad musty libraries. Come to think of it, though, I do get an inordinate number of phone calls and e-mails from them seeking the last word on matters of grammar and spelling!

CHAPTER FIVE

It would be an unforgivable distortion of truth to present only the staff-sergeant dimension of Mother's role in my young life. In some notable areas she was as lax as she was rigid in others. One of these had to do with my cuisine of choice, which bore little resemblance to customary fare in our household. Eggs, however they were prepared, came right back up in my plate. Perhaps that was why she did not press me unduly to eat anything else I had a mind to refuse, and I refused a wide range of edibles indeed, some of which are popularly held to be essential for normal development—if not survival itself. I would as soon have died as get a piece of fat or chicken skin in my mouth, and I still eschew Chinese food on that very account. I don't eat what I can't clearly identify.

That's not so bad, but I also avoided all green vegetables and most other colors and acquired an intense dislike for milk. Since cake usually contains both eggs and milk, Mother reasoned that I could get those nutrients thus disguised, so it wasn't unusual for my meals to begin with dessert if that was what I wanted. The cake didn't even have to be baked as far as I was concerned, for I considered the batter to be ambrosia of the gods. I still recall Mother's going to the kitchen at nine o'clock one night just to stir up some at my behest.

I did like chocolate milk. Mother treated me to a half-pint bottle of it one winter day. I stuck it outside in the snow to chill and in due time went back to retrieve it. In the process, I dropped it on the sidewalk and smashed one whole side of the top. Undaunted, I drank from the other side. When I walked in sipping from the nearly empty broken container, Mother gasped appropriately and clutched the region of her heart, visualizing slivers of glass penetrating my innards at that very instant. The fact that she survived my childhood is more astonishing than the fact that I did.

Left to my own culinary devices, I did all right. Peanut butter was a staple, and I ate it combined with light corn syrup as a spread for sandwiches or plain with sliced sweet pickles. (They keep it from sticking to the roof of the mouth.) Bread crusts were routinely cut off until a fellow student in the sixth grade made fun of my neatly trimmed lunch-box entrees and said my teeth would all fall out as a consequence of this idiosyncrasy. He probably had a repository of Didactic Gems somewhere in his background too. They didn't—fall out, that is—but maybe I reformed just in the very nick. I also like baked sweet potatoes with mustard and salt-cured ham (very, very lean ham) fried to the color and texture of beef jerky. That could have made up for the bread crusts.

Tapioca was on my taboo list, possibly because of its resemblance to raw egg whites, so when strawberries were in season, Anamary always made two pies: one with tapioca for everybody else, one without for me. I couldn't even watch when my father ate pickled pigs' feet.

Both meals and bedtimes sort of scheduled themselves along the lines of natural inclination. There was no irksome regimentation to speak of. I stayed up until the adults went to bed. Neither Mother nor Anamary ate an evening meal (such a practice was believed to interfere with their sleep), and Dad was frequently gone. My supper was therefore always served on demand.

Best of all, I was permitted to roam at will on my uncles' farms when we visited them, summoned back by the car horn when it was time to leave. Dresses had a way of attaching themselves to every barbed-wire fence I crawled through, so it wasn't unusual for me to show up not only dirty, but also on the ragged side of intact. This was apparently accepted as part of my initiation into the joys of roughing it, so these things went unremarked. There was a rather annoying ritual Anamary and I went through without fail before I set out on my rambles. It began with "Let me fix your hair first" and ended with "Watch out for snakes." I think she just fussed with my hair to be certain she had time to get in the snake warning, since nobody was going to see me but the livestock and I always returned with ribbons askew and curls uncurled anyway.

Her cautionary advice was unnecessary. Even without it, I would have kept a sharp eye out on my surroundings. So sharp, in fact, that I sometimes stood motionless and transfixed for long minutes at a time staring at suspicious looking black sticks before I dared even to breathe. You don't know the meaning of "stock still" unless you've been stared down sometime by a stick.

If the "stick" moved, then so did I, naturally. Mercury's heels had nothing on mine when that happened. I was painting on a creek bank one time, intent upon my work, when my Scot terrier, who had accompanied me, sat down on one end of a stick whose other end happened to lie just inside my peripheral vision less than an arm's length away. When it suddenly reared up, so did I. This was the closest I have ever come to self-levitation.

"Sticks" didn't always really have to move to move me. I trailed along with a cousin once as a child when she went to drive in the cows one evening. While we were thus occupied, her older brother killed a snake and stretched its remains across the lane down which we had to return.

When Bea and I came upon the *corpus delecti*, our reactions were somewhat different. She began looking for a stout cudgel with which to kill the critter (again), and I headed back down the lane in the opposite direction at break-neck speed. Presently I heard feet pounding behind me to the accompaniment of much unintelligible shouting, which I took as encouragement to be even more fleet of foot. I supposed the snake was after the lot of us. My sole concern was to go wherever that road took me with all possible haste.

At last the practical joker caught up and managed to bring me to a halt by running me into the brambles in the fencerow. I looked back then, expecting to find the snake within striking distance. Instead, here came the entire family like a string of geese, Anamary bringing gamely up the rear and the whole kit and kaboodle as winded from laughing as from running.

"Where in the world were you going?" puffed Bea's dad when he reached me.

"Away," I puffed back.

The prankster on this occasion was one and the same rascal who introduced me to the incomparable delights of green persimmons and swore that taking hold of an electric fence wouldn't affect me if I held it with both hands. Incidentally, fence currents never affected Anamary in the least. I even saw her pull off her shoes and stand barefoot on the ground one time to prove that her soles were not insulating her from shock as she calmly held the charged wire. While a young girl, she was once standing at the doorway during a storm when a bolt of lightning shot through it and grazed her on the shoulder. Maybe that experience altered the electromagnetic property of her body in some way. Who knows?

As an aside to those naturalists who get up in arms at the mention of killing a snake, let me explain that some snakes in my native state are venomous. One of them, the copperhead, doesn't even coil to strike. A sudden *zap* and you've had it—no rattle, no hiss, no counting to ten to give you a head start. Two of the Frank boys were bitten by copperheads as young men. They didn't die, but they became awfully sick. Claud plowed one up and was struck right through a split in his shoe over his little toe. Marvin was also plowing on a separate occasion and was bitten just above his shoe top. Claud recovered enough to go to a dance the same night, but nothing short of the Grim Reaper's scythe could have prevented that.

Another Missouri viper, the cottonmouth (or water moccasin), looks very much like some of its nonpoisonous cousins until it opens its giveaway jaws. I never figured it was too smart to ask a snake to say "Ahhhh" just to check out its family tree.

Even the so-called "harmless" serpents that supposedly rid farmers of unwanted rodents also rid them of wanted things like eggs and baby chickens. One of their favorite hangouts is therefore the chicken house. Dad's father was pecked by an ill-tempered hen one time when he was gathering up eggs. Believing he was snake-bit, he all but expired before the truth became apparent. Heart failure can be as fatal as poison.

"Dad's father"—a curious phrase, to be sure. That brings up one of the more interesting consequences of adoption (mine, anyway). Because it was known that an adopted girl in Poplar Bluff had killed herself on learning about her ersatz identity at eighteen, I was told about mine almost as soon as I learned to talk. It's one of the earliest memories I have. I can still see exactly where I was standing by the living-room heater and where Mother was sitting playing idly with something in her hands—maybe a rubber band. Putting it in terms of her wanting me while my own mother didn't set me up for some emotional scars that I probably still carry, but it was a well-intentioned blunder, and I don't hold it against her. Adoptive parents are coached now to be more sensitive to the damage such a statement can inflict. I hope so, at least. I would have trouble with relationships for many years because I doubted that proffered love was genuine, that I was worthy of it somehow. Rejection by the person most endowed by Nature to give unconditional devotion and to defend a child to the very death can be an enormously crippling burden to the psyche.

But, to continue, there was no love lost between Mother and her in-laws, particularly her father-in-law. Whatever his early history of riotous debauchery, I knew him as a gentle little man who always managed to have a peppermint about him when I showed up. The worst I can personally testify to is the sometimes rather tall and self-aggrandizing yarns he spun on and on until he wife shut him up with a volley of the most creative expletives I've ever heard. I still regret that I didn't write them down for future reference.

He was a small, gaunt man, half Irish and half Cherokee Indian. The combination created an interesting visage: coal-black, straight hair, dark skin, high cheekbones, and rather steely blue eyes. His lineage reflects the history of the railroads as they crossed our nation's midsection. Immigrant Irishmen whose labor pushed the iron horse westward often took Indian wives as their work brought them into contact with The Nations. Charlie wore a heavy, drooping mustache that dripped coffee at mealtimes, and he ate peas with a knife. I was always fascinated by that art and longed to try it myself, hindered only by the fact that peas are green vegetables. He was also virtually deaf—except when people whispered what they didn't want him to know.

Whether it was true or not, I can't say, but Charlie Brannon claimed credit for instigating the use of cinders on railroad beds to keep them intact. He was a section foreman when tracks were being laid in the bottoms of "Swampeast Missouri," where washouts were a constant frustration. Long before I knew him, he allegedly kept a big barrel of whiskey on hand in the barn lot, and as a young lad, my father was often sent out with a lantern after dark to walk the rails and look for Charlie in case he was lying across them somewhere in a drunken slumber.

Dad's mother, Betty, was as broad as her husband was thin. She was of Dutch extraction and married Charlie when she was only thirteen. She smoked a pipe and dipped snuff and handled the family's money like a Swiss banker though she never learned to read or write. She could have been the prototype of Martha Hoople, especially as regards her ongoing crusade against her husband's use of demon rum. Just when she thought she had cured him of his habit, his brother came to stay a while. There was a handy knothole in the wall of a room that faced the barn. When she wasn't looking through it to spy on their shenanigans, it was concealed by a picture. One day she caught the two taking a nip. Upstairs she went, threw her brother-in-law's belongings into his trunk, and heaved it out the window. He got the message.

Tramps caught the brunt of her ire too. One appeared at the kitchen window one day where she was washing dishes. Screens were unheard of. He asked for a handout and, not liking her response, informed her that was no way to speak to a gentleman.

"I'll 'gentleman' you, you son of a bitch!" she replied and flung the whole pan of dishwater in his face. He, too, got the message.

She had a good arm. A kerosene lamp somehow caught on fire one night. Running to the door with it, she lobbed it into the night air. It went end over end and came to rest sitting upright on a fence post.

Then there was the story my dad loved to tell about the time when food was becoming scarce and his mother grabbed the shovel and told him to come along with her (in his perennial role as lantern bearer). Into the wilderness they marched. Suddenly a mink jumped out from under a log. The shovel came down swift and sure, and the pelt brought enough to relieve their famine. This was a day when panthers could still occasionally be heard screaming in the swamps and normally courageous dogs often refused to hunt far from their human companions. Wolves once allegedly ate a man in the area who'd been injured felling a tree. His buddies had placed him in a hollow log for protection while they went to get help. Some protection.

Times were somewhat better, of course, when I first became fully acquainted with Betty. Her vegetable garden was always a wonder to behold. Anything she stuck in the ground would grow and flourish, so her table was usually well laden. Unfortunately, she had a habit of tasting things right out of the pot while she cooked—the only way to get it right if you can't read a recipe. This custom was not regarded as sanitary by Mother and Anamary, so when civility demanded and we were obliged to eat at the senior Brannons', one or both of my guardian angels hung around the kitchen and helped prepare the meal or else kept an eye peeled for violations of FDA guidelines. Then I would be taken aside and given the benefit of a secretive "It's okay to eat the potatoes, but don't touch the gravy" kind of warning. The message I really got was that only those germs belonging to an alien clan are harmful.

It backfired, of course. Mother forgot that her clan was alien to me as well. Nobody ever seemed to notice that when we visited them, I only drank water when a fresh bucket was drawn from the well and I got to the dipper in common use before anyone else did. Jay Walter did detect a kindred practice and marveled about it as long as he lived, but he went to his grave ignorant of what lay behind it. I always gouged butter from the middle of the mound instead of the side where everyone else carved his portion—usually with his fork.

So profound was Mother's disapproval of her in-laws that I was instructed not to identify with them in any manner whatsoever. Thus denied the use of appellations appropriate to Dad's progenitors, I was in a considerable bind if I wanted to refer to them or address one of them directly. This served wonderfully to reinforce my awareness that adoption set me apart. It would have been unthinkable to call them Charlie and Betty, so I was always regarded as an extraordinarily quiet child in their presence, and people who didn't know better were left with the impression that I didn't have any living grandparents. Actually, they both survived well into my adulthood.

Mother began her crusade of separating the sheep from the goats so early, in fact, that by the time I was about two, I went around asserting defiantly that I was *"not* Doshune Bannno" but, rather, "Dune Dune Fank." That must have delighted my father to no end. Because I shortly refused to answer to "Dorris" at all, the family, needing to communicate with me fairly frequently, finally capitulated and merely called me "June"—or "Junie Baby" in Mother's case. Until she died.

Under the circumstances, it might have been well had Mother stuck to her original impulse to name me "Ruth Ann," especially since people all over the country where I have lived—both strangers and those who knew me intimately—have persisted in calling me *Ruth* inadvertently. Never *Jean* or *Joan* or *Jane* as one would logically expect. It has not merely been a slip of the tongue, either. A friend of many years moved away and addressed her first letter to me as *Ruth*, and a professor I had once gave me a book at the end of a term I had spent in his class, inscribing it "To *Ruth*."

Another eerie incident occurred when a correspondent whom I had never met began his first missive to me with "Dear June" (directly under my correct full name and address) and then started the second paragraph with "You, *Ruth*, have offered to help me." This blew my previous theory that the phenomenon had something to do with associating certain names with certain personalities. I have even been introduced by an acquaintance as "Dorris Ruth." Perhaps all these people knew me as a *Ruth* in some previous shared lifetime.

It may seem to those with black sheep in their flock or unsightly skeletons in a closet here and there that being able to pick and choose relatives at will is an attractive state of affairs. I'm not so sure it's a boon. Claiming kin to whomever I pleased and retreating behind my adoption when I didn't please left me without a "given" to which I had to accommodate my ego and allowed me to construct in fantasy a family tree of such perfection it would have been in a class by itself in the Garden of Eden. Plutarch was certainly right when he observed that the glory belongs to our ancestors if we're well descended (and, conversely, the shame if we're not), but most of us forget that now and again.

I made allowances for my birth mother and imagined her beautiful to compensate for her obvious moral shortcomings. I must have intuited a profound secret, for I took a criminology course at the University of Arizona one summer in which the following true/false question appeared on the final: "If a woman is beautiful, she doesn't have to be good." I still haven't a clue as to what our ring-a-ding professor considered the right choice. Distrusting males in general along then, I decided the better part of valor was to remain ignorant of his rationale. I answered it "False," but I've had a sneaky suspicion ever since that I got it wrong. After all, this wasn't a course in ethics or the history of religion. Heaven only knows where sociologists are coming from. I certainly don't. That is not to say I know where most representatives of religion are coming from, though I have a few good guesses.

One cousin with whom I had no qualms about identifying was Ellen, eight years my senior. Claud, her father, had stayed on with Grandma and Anamary to tend the farm, living in a little house across a field from them after he married. When Grandma died and Anamary came to stay with us, he and his family moved into their place, and the temporary dwelling was claimed by the wild plums and persimmons. The age differential was without consequence—to me. What forbearance Ellen had to employ is her secret to this day. I got her out of doing a lot of dishes, though, since excusing her also got me out from under foot.

Our favorite place to play was a miniature "Grand Canyon" that had developed in one corner of the farm in the same manner as its larger counterpart—from years of erosion. The configuration was the same. Buttes and ravines alternated in a labyrinthine pattern of light and shadow. Fingers of hard but gravely soil came to ridges too sharp to sit on, much less walk, or accommodated small tufted plateaus that served beautifully as lookout points for explorers or Indians or whoever was "it" in a game of hide-and-seek. Unless, of course, the person who was not "it" cheated and walked backwards in her own footprints to some crevice out of bounds, concealed even from the keen eyes of hawks that wheeled overhead in search of lone chickens stupidly straying too far from the protection of the .22 hanging over Claud's front door. Hawks do catch full-grown chickens, regardless of the lengths traversed by conservationists to revise and edit the creatures' reputation.

Like most Paradises, the Big Ditches (as opposed to the Little Ditches closer to the house) could only be approached by torturous means. One had to brave oceans of bitter-smelling dog fennel, which tended to get caught between the toes, and beggars' lice (a plant whose seed is a small fuzzy burr that sticks like Super Glue to anything remotely resembling fabric), not to mention saw-briars that left careless ankles laced with beads of blood. It was not a terrain for the faint of heart or the tender of foot. Pity the child who never knew such hazards or such rewards for his pain. This flora serves a useful evolutionary purpose in the cause of the fittest man's survival, I'm certain. It forces one to look at the ground as he walks along, thereby enabling him to avoid—what else?—snakes.

I grew up with another danger too that now gives me a few goosebumps. When I was eight years old, we moved about seventy-five miles to Jackson, Missouri, the county seat of Cape Girardeau County, where Dad worked on a branch line that permitted him to spend every night at home and eat all his meals there. The "Milkcan Special" made two round trips per weekday to Allenville, going on to Delta on Wednesdays. This schedule made it possible for me to tag along at will during summer vacations. I had the run of the caboose and often rode on the platform at the end, watching the tracks converge at their vanishing point, all but mesmerized by the clickity-clack of the wheels that sang like living, wordless poetry in my youthful ear. Dad was a brakeman and was therefore idle between stops. He never lectured me about being careful, but I remember now with a full and grateful heart how often I turned to go back inside the coach and found him peering out the little window in the door. Goodness knows how many miles and hours he spent in those watchful vigils.

Sometimes a can of cream left too long in the sun for the arrival of the train literally blew its top. That was always a treat. And then there was the assortment of things shipped, from boa constrictors to turkey chicks. Dad gave me one that had been injured in transit once. Named Hop-Along (as in Cassidy) because of his limp, he made a wonderful pet until he met an untimely death, probably from a surfeit of flies I obligingly swatted for him.

Aside from the fact that Dad became identified in my mind with trains in general (he began working on the section gang building and repairing tracks at thirteen), there are specific associations between him and his occupation that I particularly cherish. To stop the train, the brakeman had only to "pull the air" back in the coach or caboose. Once he did this to free a dog caught in a barbed-wire fence along the right-of-way. Another time he halted the train to pull up a bushel basketful of wildflowers for Mother to plant around the house. What the Goulds and Morgans of the world would have said about such use of company time is not difficult to imagine, but man, indeed, does not live by bread alone. That which makes one a better person also makes him a better employee—a fact all but lost in our impersonal, technological age.

My father had been dead about a year when I arranged with the conductor of the same branch line on which he had worked till retirement to take my three young sons on a sentimental journey from Jackson to Allenville, where my husband was to meet us with the car. But when I boarded the caboose, the past was too much with me. The guardian presence that should have been there was missing, and the pain was too acute. I stood on the familiar platform, engulfed in the combined odor of oil and steel and cinders, leaned my head against the toddler I was holding and sobbed. The trip was postponed indefinitely.

I'm not sure I would have trusted my boys with the same freedom I enjoyed on my childhood jaunts by rail. But when we backed over crossings, I was allowed to toot the whistle on the rear end, and that was worth considerable risk.

It was a beautiful, glorious, *intimate* time to be alive and very young. Who would be king of all he surveys when he could be part of it as I was and feel that affinity in his very bones? It was a time of sitting on front porches and knowing all the neighbors (and everything they did), of leaving doors unlocked through the day and walking dark streets after thirty-five-cent movies unafraid, of buying drugs only in drug stores and eggs in brown paper bags. My world was free of plastic refuse and powered lawn mowers, and it is gone for good.

Every adult creates his own romance with the past, but surely it is getting harder to do now than it was for my generation. The longer I live, the more important that process becomes. How terribly sad that many parents today seem intent on giving their children *things* instead of *memories*. Things don't last; memories do. I can't recall half the dolls I had, but I can rebuild in minute detail the stick barns and houses Ellen and I once erected in the sand at the edge of the woods and the stick wagons full of acorn "watermelons" that we pushed to market or stored in cellars of our own careful construction. Surely the recent Elian Gonzalez fiasco marks the nadir of Western materialism. That so very many Americans could equate a child's best interest with his potential for eating hot dogs and owning toys directly reflects the degree to which we have sold out to Mammon. The mother who works not to put food on the table and clothes on her children's backs but to put a second car in the garage and a spa on her patio is an agent of that sellout.

One of the reasons I always loved visiting Ellen in the country was the fact that her father never owned a car and never felt deprived. Every Saturday the family piled into the hack on spring seats and rode to town behind a team of horses to do the week's "trading"—eggs and cream for staples like flour and sugar. When I was privileged to be part of this custom, I looked down upon the automobiles that passed us with disdain mitigated only by the merest hint of pity. And when Claud trusted me with the reins on backcountry roads, I wouldn't have exchanged places with crowned heads of Europe.

Nor was there electricity in the old home place. There are no other shadows like those cast by kerosene lamps on summer nights or a fireplace in winter. They lived discrete lives behind a table here, a chair there, merging into the tapestry of talk that droned on about times long past. Only the call of a distant whippoorwill kept them rooted in the present. For the prudent child struggling to stay awake so as to forestall banishment to the lonely darkness of bed, listening was a mere adjunct of watching these otherworldly intruders come and go in a strange dimension they themselves somehow created. It didn't seem terribly safe to take one's eye off them for very long.

It was a different century I was permitted to glimpse, and I loved its mystery and, at the same time, its marvelous simplicity. I loved the music of cowbells drawing closer at milking time and the way the earth itself seemed to listen to night coming on. In such a hush, I can still remember standing awestruck in Claud's lane one evening, hearing only the beat of my own heart and knowing a oneness with the Universe—as trite as that sounds—that may never come again in this lifetime. The moment passed, like the one Moley and Rat knew in their search for the young otter, but it so outshined the many hours I have since spent in various houses of "worship" that these were foreordained to leave me disappointed and unimpressed. Whatever the *soul* may be, mine reached out in that twilight to its Source, through the very stuff of which it is made and will ever remain a part.

Is it to find that stillness now that so many kids do drugs? Is it a desperate search for peace in chaos, for silence in cacophony? "The old order changeth, yielding place to new," as Tennyson declares, "and God fulfills Himself in many ways / Lest one good custom should corrupt the earth." It seems to this bystander that perhaps some customs were less corrupting than those which have replaced them.

We're still *waiting for Godot*, and *Moshiach will be here this year*—every year for decades and centuries on end. Yet we continue to live in spite of evidence to the contrary as if there will be no next year to face in its prosaic realities. "Take no thought for the morrow" was not good advice when it was given, and it still isn't. Collectively we are paying the price because individually too many persist in imagining otherwise, whether out of religious wishful thinking or self-indulgent withdrawal from active participation in trying to better today, the only real thread from which tomorrow has ever been or ever will be woven.

CHAPTER SIX

Of a naturally open and curious mind, I checked out an elderly psychic in St. Louis many years ago on the recommendation of someone who actively participated in experiments involving paranormal phenomena conducted by a group whose nucleus formed around the late John Neihardt of *Black Elk Speaks* fame. These have been well documented by John Thomas Richards in *SORRAT*, a comprehensive survey of results the group obtained at Neihardt's Skyrim Farm near Columbia, Missouri. The Rev. Mrs. Leona Boyles, who had used her "second sight" to locate Jed Smith's grave for Neihardt, was a character in her own right. Her mother had been a Gypsy who plied her fortune-telling trade door to door. Sometimes the "magic" worked, and sometimes it didn't. When it didn't, she faked a pretty good substitute and taught her daughter to do the same.

Leona seldom had to fake it, however. Her gift was genuine and as little understood by her as by anyone else. She combined with it a conveniently tailored practice of Roman Catholicism, thus producing a hybrid bastard religion that would probably have been at home in the pre-Christian glades of Tuscany. The Sanhedrin would have done her to death, as would the Inquisitional Dominicans and the Puritans and all the other righteous cowards who have cloaked their inordinate fear of weird old women in the mantle of Divine Wrath. I found her fascinating and delightful. This whole preamble, however, is merely by way of stating what she said to me when I walked in.

Giving me a long penetrating look, she declared, "There's something very strange about you." Coming from a considerable authority on strange females, that was quite a mouthful. I could do little but laugh my acknowledgement of her perspicacity.

All other oddities aside (and they are legion), one that most discomfits my more conventional acquaintances concerns my flirtations with the metaphysical in a uniquely ecumenical array of its sundry *apologias*. They begin, again, with the unusual circumstances of my adoption.

The Brannons and all but one of the Frank boys had no religious affiliation whatsoever. Church doings in rural Stoddard County served—as in many another locale—more prominently as a social outlet than a spiritual one. Young men attended them to be allowed to walk home this or that girl, and the girls went to be walked home. Sermons may have had some incidental salutary effect on the conduct they all maintained en route, but that's debatable. Where high moral standards prevailed, they were largely acquired in the home.

There had been some Lutheran leanings way back in the Germanic Frank clan, but those had been left behind in the Old Country. John and Vany sang hymns with their children and read aloud from the family Bible, interpreting it to their individual needs and according to their individual insights, which were predicated upon common sense and generous and loving natures. However little they had, no one was ever turned away from their door hungry or, if shelter was needed for the night, without a place to sleep.

Perhaps because of the earlier Lutheran conservatism or the flavor of Southern gentility that Vany brought to the heritage from antebellum days, Mother and Anamary—and their brothers too— looked considerably askance at the carryings-on of the fundamentalist Protestants in communities scattered about the hills of Crowley's Ridge, and when ministers, having whipped their flocks into the appropriate emotional frenzy, called upon those among their congregations who were "saved" to rise and declare the fact before God and man, Mother and Anamary stoically remained seated. They considered their spiritual well-being to be nobody else's business except to the degree that their daily lives and their interactions with others provided ample testimony.

This passive approach to collective worship, as it filtered down to me, gave church-going the status of a spectator sport. Twice I was hustled from the midst of the Elect on account of laughing out loud at the proceedings. This was before I learned that stoicism should properly extend to amusement as well as one's state of grace. The first indiscretion happened at a tent revival. Its similarity to a circus went far beyond the tarp and sawdust. At the point where hysteria took over, a very fat old lady joined the shouters and literally danced up and down the aisles, shaking like a bowl of Jello in a 7.5 earthquake, waving her arms and shrieking what I take now to have been hosannas in a subdialect of Swahili. Maybe it wasn't the Greatest Show on Earth, but it certainly entertained me.

The second breach of church etiquette occurred on foot-washing Sunday at Hills Church near three of my uncles. It was the usual white cracker box set in a grove of hickory trees. But for its want of a steeple it could have come off any down-home calendar for the month of October. This was the annual date set aside for the preacher, in replication of Christ's humility, to wash the feet of those among the membership who wished to be thus ministered to. One by one they came forward to the raised platform that constituted the "sanctuary." All went well till he got to a stout old sister with ticklish tootsies. No sooner had he laid hold on a bare size ten and a half foot than she let out a whoop, kicked up her heels, and upset the pan, giving the humble servant of God an uncalculated drenching. My spontaneous reaction barely masked some very adult titters and a lot of sudden coughing.

While we still lived in Poplar Bluff, my most frequent exposure to what passed for religion took place at a hole-in-the-wall ministry called "The Mission." The "man of the cloth" there happened to be a female firecracker with flaming red hair, a characteristic of which she was proud because Jesus was supposedly (according to some Aryan reports) a blue-eyed titian blond himself. That's about as likely as frostbite in the Sahara. A sign in the storefront-type window proclaimed The Mission to be "nondenominational," meaning that it defied resemblance to every known sectarian organization and probably went all the way back in recorded history to the day when the Reverend Kitty got the call.

The church had two prominent features: a large galvanized baptismal tank behind the podium and a huge cross of red crepe paper stretched over a wooden frame. The latter was lit up from inside when the occasion necessitated dramatic effect. It was always lit when I sang solos *a cappella* in front of it, holding my arms out to mimic its configuration. My voice then, before the ravages of bronchiectasis all but did it in, was a clear contralto. That, combined with my childhood innocence (if children are, in fact, ever innocent), was a sure bet to draw penitents to the mourners' bench in veritable droves while women wept and "talked in tongues" or jumped around shouting. It wasn't lost on me that the Holy Ghost could be always be counted upon to descend on the very same people every time and that the choice bore no correlation to the known purity of the beneficiaries' lives the other six days of the week. All the Christians I have ever known, bar none, practice selective reading of the Good Book; otherwise, some of these zealots would have blundered upon St. Paul's admonition to the Corinthians that they keep quiet when so moved unless another person is present to interpret the message in the common vernacular.

I began "performing" at The Mission before I could read, memorizing verses of hymns at home under Mother's or Anamary's tutelage. After a piano was bought for me at four, I played by ear and accompanied myself. That brought every wino in off the streets for blocks around and prompted several to be born again—and again and again. I eventually got bored with this diversion and had to be bribed to continue. Hence my rather large collection of dolls.

Although Dad sometimes risked hearing a sermon on the topic of adultery and accompanied us, it was normally only the womenfolk who went to church with any regularity. A fellow trainman by the name of Gene Sells was a self-designated minister of the Gospel, however, and he occasionally prevailed upon Dad to attend his church. He also had a weekly radio service at which I once sang standing on a chair in order to reach the microphone.

I always gave the Reverend Mr. Sells my rapt attention—so rapt I was pointed out to other children as the ultimate model of preferred behavior in the House of the Lord. Nobody knew that I was merely determined not to miss what I considered momentarily imminent: to wit, that Mr. Sells would stomp the floor so hard when he really got wound up that he'd go through it just like Rumpelstiltskin. He often literally frothed at the mouth, spittle raining out like the fire and brimstone he predicted were soon to descend on all us poor sinners. I was glad we habitually sat near the back. This was no Bible thumper; this was a genuine Bible *pounder*, whose diatribes wandered all over both Testaments and ended up resembling neither except for the "thee's" and "thou's." May he rest in more peace than he promised others.

Given this background, what came next still baffles me. It is the granddaddy of *non-sequiturs*. I was sent to a Catholic school. Mother claimed it was because she didn't trust the public school system, not so much in terms of education as peer influence, but there had to have been some hidden agenda somewhere. Maybe she knew it would cause Charlie Brannon, a Mason from way back, to worry the ends off his mustache with nervous fingers that itched to strangle her. Or maybe Fate just stepped in again, as Fate will now and then, and it only seemed like a matter of choice.

Well, whatever. As for me, I couldn't have been happier. Nuns in their black habits and starched white wimples and priests in their long cassocks were right down my alley, since they took the mundane and elevated it to the romantic and mystical where things spiritual rightly belong. Holy Mother Church *really* lost her grip on the not-so-faithful when she began looking and acting like John Doe Baptist at a camp meeting. But, as we've already noted, the old order changeth. I performed in a benefit program in Cape

Girardeau back in the 70s when the Sisters of St. Francis were trying to raise funds towards construction of a new hospital. The nuns had discarded their habits several years before, but that night the administrator wore the full traditional regalia. It brought down the house with a standing ovation. I can assure you it was the garb, not the woman, inspiring that enthusiastic response born of nostalgic yearning.

The only codicil Mother insisted upon was my not being obliged to participate in catechism classes. It was a pyrrhic victory, for I was there in the flesh and listened to everyone else being drilled. I just didn't get a grade for what I learned. I sometimes went to Mass, however, and often paid brief visits to church during recesses, for my aesthetically starved little soul had found a home. How different the majestic beauty of the altar and the stained glass, the ambience of incense mingled with deep, quiet shadows cast by lifelike statuary from the carnival atmosphere of what I had known as "church." There is a bit of Scripture somewhere that reads to the effect of "be still and know that I am God." That message and its implications have apparently been lost on a lot of people. Joseph Campbell understood the role of awe in the healthy functioning of the human psyche and tried over the course of his adult life to share that understanding with a society ever more desperately in need of it. His was one of the most compelling voices of the Twentieth Century, but it has largely been drowned out by the ranks of fundamentalists who seem to think public demonstration is evidence of inner spirit and that all we must do is hang up the Ten Commandments and blast prayer out over PA systems to change the world. Sigh.

Although mine was as liberal and tolerant a family as could have been found in the Brannons' socioeconomic niche, Mother made it clear that I was not to become a Catholic, and I remember reading a ballad on fragile yellow paper that had been handed down through several generations of Franks that was to Roman Catholicism what *Protocols of the Elders of Zion* was to Judaism. I had already become sufficiently indoctrinated to find it highly offensive and patently false. Its heroine fell under the sway of some foul "Romish" plot, and she ended very badly. I wish to goodness I could still lay my hand on that piece of calumny, for it would be quite valuable now.

Had I been forgetful of the proscription under which I was being educated, occasional reminders would have served to refresh my memory. Once, for example, a classmate who had taken a particular liking to me gave me her rosary, a lovely thing with pale green glass beads. Suspecting what would happen when Mother found out, I tried to decline it, but nothing doing. It must be mine. Too honest to be clandestine about it but not quite honest enough to be truthful either, I mulled over my dilemma all the way home that day and finally hit on the perfect subterfuge—I thought. I put it around my neck and swore and be damned it was a necklace. Nice try. Back it went to my friend, who was only slightly less crushed than I.

My first year at Sacred Heart was educational in more ways than anticipated. I learned about prejudice first hand. Read Chaim Potok and you'd think only Jews ever got beat up for being incubated in the wrong wombs. Never mind poor bloody Ireland. I had the unique pleasure of being attacked merely because it was observed by certain ruffians that my daily perambulations took me to a Catholic school. They became so convincingly menacing that I finally decided to arm myself, and on the very day that I went forth—like another small combatant—with rocks in my pockets, they waylaid me and blocked my progress any farther along the sidewalk. They were all boys, of course, and bigger than I. I was ready. I fetched out my weapons and threatened to split open their skulls. Just then a "big girl" happened upon the scene and inquired into the matter. When I told her the trouble, she shooed the Philistines back into their yard and watched me safely down the block and out of sight. But I was not disposed to depend upon on fortuitous rescues anymore, so after that, Anamary always walked me to and from school.

The injustice of the scenario would have been every bit as real had I actually been a christened, dyed-in-the-wool Catholic, but the moral I gleaned from it was never to draw conclusions from appearances only. It has stood me in very good stead ever since.

I loved school and cried because I couldn't go on Saturdays and Sundays. Mother Perpetua was all the saints rolled into one. She also reminded me of my recently deceased grandmother, whom I had also adored. Trying to please her was all the motivation I needed to learn. Talking in class was my perennial undoing in spite of this, and I still smart when I remember the worst "discipline" I ever suffered at her hands. I must have been extraordinarily exasperating one day, for she bent a stern look upon me and exclaimed, "June! You provoke me so!" That was enough. To think I had driven so gentle a creature to such an extreme humiliated me beyond expression. I was probably speechless for the next thirty minutes at least.

From Mother Perpetua I went to Mother Boniface, who was younger and who ruled the third grade with a very firm resolution to wrest from each child the best that was in him. We wrote with fountain pens and ink then, and I thought myself very ill-used because I sometimes had to stay in after school to copy over sloppy papers. She knew I could do better, and she made me do it. Therein lies the secret. I chafed, but I persevered. When she bent to give me a hug and a kiss along with my report card the day I was leaving for good to move to Jackson, she whispered in my ear, "Don't forget what I have taught you." And I haven't, though at the time I didn't know what it was I had learned. Some lessons are like that.

My status in Jackson was even stranger than it had been in Poplar Bluff, where there were a few other non-Catholics, most of them "hopeless" cases who had been kicked out of the public school. My enrollment at Immaculate Conception coincided with the parish's maiden voyage into parochial education, so I was the only non-Catholic pupil, but the only one who had ever attended a Catholic school before. Initially, our classes met in the convent, from which we were shortly moved into a two-room building that accommodated four grades per room with only two Teaching Sisters of Notre Dame to carry on.

Far from impoverishing the quality of our education, this arrangement actually enhanced it. In each room, the older children had the benefit of reviewing daily what the younger ones were just learning, and the younger students could, by the same token, pick up a lot they would later need by listening to what was being taught the older ones. It was no accident that when the public school districts began consolidating and eliminated small country schools organized in the same way, the students thus engulfed displayed, across the board, a considerable edge over their theoretically more privileged city counterparts.

In addition to the superlative and dedicated teachers we had in the persons of Sisters Danielle and Alvina (who was later replaced by Sister Mary Raymond, alias "The Battle Ax"), we small girls were treated to lessons in crocheting by the housekeeping nun during noon breaks. Coming upon me in the process of raveling out a mistake during one of these sessions, the parish priest, Father Sommerhauser, adroitly observed, "As ye sew, so shall ye rip." Would to God it were that simple! No reaping tares and thistles, just ripping out the errors and doing them over the right way.

By the year I was in the sixth grade, I was coming home arguing theology with Mother, and she thought she saw the handwriting on the wall. So did I. It was time for another bit of legerdemain. I purchased the books I would need in the seventh grade before the term was up, so when the anticipated announcement came to the effect that I would not be going back there the next year, I innocently protested that I must, seeing as how I already had *spent good money* for my texts. It didn't work any better than the necklace charade. The following fall, I was packed off to Jackson Grade School. It was a milestone that even Mother would later admit regretting.

After my first day in the public school, I cried all the way home, stormed into the living room, slammed my books on the floor and screamed, "I won't go back there again if I never go to school another day in my life!" Wrong. But that didn't keep me from hating it with a black and terrible passion. I thought I had landed in hell a little ahead of schedule. Along with the regular curriculum in the Catholic school, we had learned respect not only for our elders, but for our peers. We stood anytime we were called upon to give an answer (which had better be right under those circumstances), and we entered and exited the classroom in patient, orderly single file as instructed. Now it was every man for himself and the devil take the hindmost—unless the unfortunate straggler was trampled to death underfoot, in which event I suppose the expression might still apply. So involuntary had my response become to hearing my name that I had some trouble breaking myself of leaping up. I was the object of much hilarity among my classmates. Heathens all.

For the next two years, I trod a very fine line between obstinacy and out-right rebellion. Fortunately, I had already learned what was being served up for the first time in the public school system, so I was able to coast through on little or no work. In the meantime, my health continued to deteriorate, but I had two pleasures in life that kept me going: music and my dog Wiggles. I had begun taking piano lessons at nine with Sister Danielle and continued with a private teacher after the shift in schools. I had begun playing a slide trombone in sixth grade, the fulfillment of an ambition generated by my seeing this instrument in a parade when I was five. Doctor Graham would later ask rhetorically, shaking his beautiful white head, why the hell I hadn't played a drum instead. I didn't want to, that's why, and for all the Freudians out there, I categorically deny that my choice of brass horns had anything whatsoever to do with penis envy, despite its shape and the fact that I was the only girl in Leroy Mason's band at that time to play such a thing. A boy my age from the public school began studying trombone the same fall I did. Every time Mason talked to Mother about my progress, he inevitably went on to comment about what "the other little boy" was doing. Some traditions die hard.

As my friends perforce changed, so did my forays into religion. Sooner or later I made the rounds: Methodist, Presbyterian, Baptist (Southern, of course), Evangelical and Reformed, Church of the Nazarene—even the Foursquare. I think I was sixteen or seventeen when I finally decided to become a Methodist. It seemed safe enough. At the time, baptism into that membership was accomplished by being sprinkled with a carnation dipped in water. Here were people who understood symbolism, no doubt about it. The same pastor who administered the rite also made a pass at me before long, so I was back to being a pagan again. I went to church there awhile afterwards, but only to ascertain to what sublime heights his hypocrisy might vaunt itself. I hoped to be a thorn in the side of his conscience, sitting there in my pew, looking my best sardonic look, but alas. He probably didn't have one.

On entering Washington University as a premed student in 1952 (having selected that fine institution on the basis of its noble Gothic architecture), I was exposed for the first time to myth-shattering, hard-core sciences that set afloat to sea my "house builded upon the sands" of a purely emotional need. It was a traumatic experience. The most painful learning we are ever called upon to do is *un*learning, and I had a great deal to jettison. In a last desperate attempt to believe in "life everlasting, world without end, amen," I turned back to Catholicism, and on my nineteenth birthday I was baptized again, this time at Immaculate Conception (with a bit of water poured upon my head). I was home once more—for the time being. Mother ate her crow with passably good manners and waited for the dessert. It would come. I had not run the gamut yet by a long shot.

CHAPTER SEVEN

I had a doctor for several years who often greeted me with "My God! Are you still alive?" This enigma is probably explained somewhere in the stars, but it would be a delightful conceit to imagine that Mother's unorthodox assortment of home remedies did the trick. (I personally think it was the peanut butter and pickles, though it might well have been the soda cracker and mayonnaise sandwiches.)

To put the matter in perspective, it should be recalled that penicillin was discovered by an Englishman only seven years before I was born and that its use was not widespread in America for some time afterwards. Musterol, though, has been around forever, and Mother spread that ointment very wide indeed. At the merest hint of lung congestion, here it came, topped with red wool flannel. Why red? I have no idea. I do know, however, that Gypsies use red to ward off the Evil Eye and that my chest (allergic to wool) always turned that color. Musterol is probably ninety-nine percent oil of garlic with a dash of horseradish thrown in as the *coup de grace*. It *will* open the sinuses, clear to the toes and out the top of the head, although its effect is not quite so instantaneous as freshly squeezed juice of garlic inserted into the nostrils. I tried this treatment once (emphasis on *once*) at the suggestion of a friend in Pittsburgh who had gotten it from a native of India. My response to the self-administered therapy rivaled that of Tom Sawyer's cat when dosed with Aunt Polly's medicinal concoction. I shot straight into the air from a prone position, did a dance all the way to the bathroom that entailed repeatedly lifting one leg very high, and stuck my head under the cold-water faucet.

I always dreaded the "Stick out your tongue" routine when I was a child. Mine never seemed to be the required color on these occasions. What followed was a regimen of Nash's Chill Tonic, a gritty, dark brown solution that I referred to as "Ashes," a much apter name. It was another patent medicine that turned me against milk: Calalactose came in the form of nasty-tasting pink pills that I had to wash down with something stronger than water to keep them down. Eventually, the milk used for this purpose began, in true Pavlov fashion, to assume the flavor of the medicine all by itself.

For someone who couldn't even stand to smell fish cooking, much less eat them, cod-liver oil was—well, never mind. Castor oil, even given in orange juice, came right back up, so Mother finally abandoned it. Ditto Milk of Magnesia. She continued to ladle out quinine, though, thinly disguised in a chocolate-flavored syrup. I took enough of that to float a steamboat. There was also the turpentine on sugar. It upset my stomach so badly I normally couldn't remember what malady had precipitated its administration. Whoever coined the adage about the cure being worse than the disease had taken lots of turpentine on sugar. For the stomach upset that resulted, there was the mustard poultice (plaster)—a paste made of mustard seeds (or prepared mustard if those were unavailable)—applied to a cloth (which did not have to be red) folded over just so and placed on the bare tummy till the nausea subsided. Pregnant women afflicted with morning sickness are hereby put on notice that they need not bother trying this.

To draw out infections or splinters embedded too deep for removal with a needle, pine tar and Vaseline were applied in combination, and to remove a foreign object from the eye, a flax seed was introduced under the lid—as if one foreign object wasn't enough. But I can go one even better than that. To cure a sty on the eyelid, a black cat's tail (belonging to either gender and attached to the living owner) was rubbed across it three times. Canines and calico kitties needed not apply. If there was no black cat handy, a gold wedding band would serve, but it was rather like settling for silver plate instead of sterling.

The interesting thing is that these remedies worked for Mother and Anamary—and their mother before them. They probably got an ancestress or two burned at the stake in Merrie Olde England at one time, though by 1928, at least, such customs were tolerated and even treated quite seriously in Cornwall, where professional charmers still plied their art. W. Oldfield Howey reports their cure for sties in *The Cat in the Mysteries of Magic and Religion*:

> Stroke the eye, from the nose out, with the tail of a black cat, Saying with a stroke to each line, "I poke thee, I don't poke thee, I toke the queff that's under the 'ee. Oh, qualyway. Oh, qualyway.

As far as I'm aware, this incantation was omitted by Grandma *et. al.*, but there's no knowing now what they might have expressed *sotto voce*.

Ellen's mama, Anzel, was a non-believer and refused to permit the application of a black cat's tail to her daughter's sty-ridden eyelids. Anamary used to tell me this story with a tone of great personal satisfaction. Grandma bided her time, and when a chance arose, she pulled it off surreptitiously. The sties promptly disappeared, and Anzel made much of the fact that they had done so without feline intervention. Grandma smiled and agreed that it was wonderful, sure as you're born.

Even Anzel subscribed to yet another remedy that would raise eyebrows today. To stop an inordinate and apparently life-threatening flow of blood, someone would grab a Bible and read aloud from the sixteenth chapter of *Ezekiel*: "When I passed by thee and saw thee wallowing in thy own blood, I said unto thee, Live. Yea, when I saw thee in thy blood, I said, Live." To be efficacious, this must be repeated three times. It was employed not only on people (I mention this for the benefit of those who would argue autosuggestion), but on livestock as well that ran afoul of a barbed wire or a sharp plow.

I am living proof that it works. Not long before Mother died, I began hemorrhaging from both lungs. At first, the bleeding occurred when I bent over, then when I got up to walk, then for no reason at all. I would awaken from a deep sleep choking, literally drowning in my own vital juices. Terrifying is scarcely the word for it. I resisted going to the hospital, because at the time I had no one to take over for me at home. Besides this, I knew there was little that could be done if I did go. I couldn't afford to lose any more lung.

On the other hand, I fully realized that I was—as my doctor kept telling me over the phone—in imminent danger of bleeding to death. He put me on codeine to suppress coughing and hoped for the best.

Then one day I remembered tales from my childhood of a portion of Scripture that was useful in such a contingency. I asked Mother if she knew which one it was. She was within a month of being ninety-three and ill herself, but her head was clear. *Ezekiel*, she thought, and recited the verses in paraphrase. I read until I found the passage. She couldn't recall if the person bleeding could say it or if someone else had to, so we tried it both ways, though it was logical to assume that someone else had to do it, since cows and horses can't read. From my standpoint, this was a pretty gutsy call on some pretty high stakes, a desperate gamble, pure and simple. There was no faith involved, just hope.

Within an hour or so, the blood changed color from very bright to dark red, and the quantity abated sufficiently so that it didn't run out my nose and I could cough it up without choking and gagging. By the time I finally checked myself into the hospital a couple of days later, I was merely bringing up blood-tinged sputum, which shortly afterwards returned to its normal color. A bronchoscopy performed at that point revealed no recent lesions whatsoever, contrary to all reasonable expectations. The doctor was at a loss to explain how the bleeding started or why it stopped. I had not only quit hemorrhaging but had completely healed up.

One certain piece of evidence that there are indeed scriptural passages that can prove medically beneficial is the proscription among religious fanatics against using them for that isolated purpose. The reason advanced is that one must have faith in God alone. The ultra-Orthodox Jewish position on the subject adds another twist to the objections: special sanctity, and therefore power, supposedly inheres exclusively to the Hebrew language, and if English can get the job done, the implications are a little disquieting. The Roman alphabet, of course, descended from the Hebrew, so it would seem that vestiges of the power would have descended with it. Anyway, the question, I submit, is whether it is preferable to die praying or to live reading *Ezekiel*. Call it magic or miracle. What is religion, anyway, but a species of magic? What difference does it really make in the long run? According to David Landau, author of *Piety and Power: The World of Jewish Fundamentalism*, some of the *haredim* place a live pigeon on the navel to cure jaundice. In light of that custom, they should be extremely cautious about condemning as sacrilegious superstition any harmless act carried out by others in an attempt to exercise some incomprehensible force upon an equally incomprehensible resistance to it in an effort to alleviate real and present suffering.

There was another relief Anamary applied from the Bible. When I got burned, she would blow upon the injury in a circular clockwise fashion three times. I didn't know there was more that went with it until she wasn't around one day and I tried the cure myself. I still hurt badly, so I demanded to know why the remedy worked for her and not for me. She was very hesitant about revealing the secret, like a high priestess protecting the esoteric mysteries of her cult. When she capitulated at last, she laid upon me a solemn duty which I swore to uphold. For the life of me, I can no longer recall what it was. So much for admitting nine-year-olds to the Sisterhood. I dimly remember that the warning had something to do with not passing the secret on to any but particular kinds of people, but that's as far as I can get. The key to the remedy was silently repeating, "Many wise men and prophets have wished to know what we now see and know"—three times, of course. Three is consistently a number of great power in the occult.

I don't advocate substituting such measures as these for more conventional medical care when it's available. By the same token, however, I would warn skeptics against lightly dismissing them in dire emergencies. Who knows what manner of power lies dormant all about us that, in general use, could conceivably be counterproductive until such time as we human beings evolve into creatures of genuine good will? If that day ever comes, perhaps then it will be at the disposal of one and all.

The tendency of Judeo-Christian closed systems of dogma to attach to any extra-religious manifestation of such power an evil source, even when the effects are undeniably beneficial, is rather baffling. It boggles the mind that the cruelest catastrophes known to humankind are solemnly attributed to the will of a theoretically omnipotent and perfectly good God while the paltry relief from pain obtained now and then through non-kosher metaphysical means in denounced as the work of malevolent spirits out to lure us from the true path. For some time now, I have planned very seriously to die laughing. The question is not how this can be accomplished, but how it could possibly be avoided by any intelligent person.

Two other interesting therapeutic measures should be mentioned in passing. When a child was gasping from the paroxysmal coughing of croup, it was made to place its mouth over the spout of a kerosene can and inhale. Once. This procedure was credited with having saved my youngest uncle's life. There's no available record of how many kids it may have killed. Another common ailment among infants back then was hives. Recovery was supposedly hastened by administration of the juice from roasted onions, taken internally.

Three teas frequently brewed for sundry afflictions were slippery elm (bark from the tree), sassafras (roots from the tree), and ginger. The last was a specific for menstrual cramps. PMS sufferers might still want to give that a whirl. If it helped my mother, who only menstruated regularly the four months she was pregnant, it should help anybody. I was never troubled that way, so I wouldn't know. In a futile attempt to be prepared for my first experience with childbirth, I read a good many articles (written by men) that said labor is like "severe menstrual cramps." Ha! I have never known one single female past puberty to scream her head off every twenty-eight days.

The mention of cramps reminds me of yet another rather bizarre remedy that was commonplace in our home. Mother was plagued by terrible cramps in her feet and legs, particularly at night, so before going to sleep, she rubbed them with white gasoline in which mothballs had been soaking for a prescribed period. She must have been a delightful bedfellow. My father chain-smoked, and often in bed, so it's a matter of some astonishment to me that she never became a human torch. I went through a phase when I was three or four during which I had a foreboding that she would die soon—possibly because my dad spent an inordinate amount of time cleaning his revolver. Therefore, the first thing I did when my feet hit the floor in the morning was to run through the house to determine if she was still alive. If the hazards inhering to gasoline baths had been known to me then, I really would have been a basket case!

Additional customs not popularly known could be forever lost to posterity if not recorded somewhere, so it might as well be here. When Anamary was young, girls (excepting herself and Mother, of course) kept their complexions white by applying urine to their skin when they went outside before bedtime to relieve themselves. There are all kinds of ways to make oneself a jolly bedfellow. Because of this bit of historical trivia, I took a very dim view of bottles marked "toilet water" when I learned to read. Maybe that's why this product so often bears its identification in French.

Anamary's hair was never cut, except to be evened off at the end every so often. The "every so often" had to coincide with the waxing of the moon rather than the waning in order to ensure luxuriant growth and abundant health (balding men might want to take note). Unwanted hair, by the same token, was removed right after the full moon. She must have done something right, for her hair was beautiful. How I loved to watch her comb it, especially on cold winter nights when it flew about like a live thing, crackling from the play of static electricity that sparkled like splinters of sunlight in its cascading thickness. She never trimmed the ends with scissors, but—very carefully, to be sure—burned them off. That certainly left nothing to be used by malignant sorcerers, should any have come along at the wrong time. Anamary never explained the practice to me (I can't believe now that I was so stupid as not to press her for the rationale), but hair and nail parings have traditionally been jealously guarded against falling into the hands off ill-wishers. My guess is that someone way back when discovered that these two things continue to grow for a while after the rest of the body has given up the ghost and therefore attributed to them a life, as it were, of their own—or at least a residual part of their owner's life.

Anyone who thinks such notions went out with the Dark Ages had better think again. I offer a quotation from the *Siddur Tehilat Hashem*, according to the text of Rabbi Schneur Zalman of Liadi, the standard prayer book used in all Lubavitcher synagogues and by all Lubavitcher Jews in their homes. It is found in an excerpt from the *Shulkhan Aruch HaRav* (the codification of Jewish Law) having to do with cutting the nails as part of the prescribed preparation of one's person for the Shabbat:

> One who burns his nails is considered a *chassid*; [who does more than the letter of the law requires]; one who buries them a *tzaddik*; while one who throws them away is a *rasha* (lest a pregnant woman step on them).

A *rasha* is a wicked man, a *tzaddik* a righteous one, and a *chassid* a very holy one indeed. The basis for the precaution, as stated in *On the Essence of Chassidus* by the late Rabbi Menachem Mendel Schneerson (sometimes spelled Menahem Mendal Schneersohn), is that stepping on nail parings will cause a miscarriage. So there you have it: the perfect solution to overpopulation and the abortion controversy. Pro-Choice people can just maintain a mail-order nail-paring bank.

Buried in antiquity, there's probably a connection between Anamary's custom and the fingernail hazard mentioned above. At any rate, her practice was just a variation on a theme that is far from played out. During visits in Reno, I used to see a woman playing poker, always in the same casino. Her fingernails had apparently never been cut in her life, or certainly not within the last twenty years. They curled around like corkscrews and, had it been possible (or desirable) to lay them out straight, they would have measured a good six inches or more. I can tell you in all honesty that I would think twice about stepping on those buggers if she ever decides to part with them, and I'll never be pregnant again! They very definitely have a life of their own. Maybe they even have something to do with her winning poker hands. In any event, I'll wager few have the courage to accuse her of cheating. How she manages to avoid putting out her eyes when she eats is more than I can understand.

One more folkway that extended into my early years: birthday celebrants, adults included, were shanghaied by however many it took and put under the bed for good luck during the following year. I won't go into some of the scenarios *that* engendered.

Whether because of or in spite of the foregoing, I lived and functioned, grew and learned, loved and hated, laughed (less and less) and cried (more and more) and thus made it to Jackson High School and a freshman year that turned into an endurance test that I nearly failed.

CHAPTER EIGHT

Adolescence is bad enough, as everyone knows who has survived it, but mine was a veritable nightmare of hard chills and high fever, of overwhelming fatigue and moody withdrawal. I came home sick from school on an average of twice a week, often cutting my last class or two. The fact that I had algebra the last hour of the day is purely coincidental. I think. Correct change for cab fare was routinely left on a bookcase by the front door to cover my impromptu arrivals. Having literally grown up with a productive cough, I accepted it as I accepted the color of my eyes—that is to say, I accommodated myself to it because I had no other choice. Not knowing how it would feel to be without it, I suppose I fared better than those who are healthy and then acquire some debilitating disease.

Ancillary problems started besetting me, though. In addition to the increasing frequency of the afternoon chills, my jaws would often lock, and only after much painful manipulation could I get my mouth open or closed, as the case might be. Eating a hamburger was a real adventure. Every cloud has a silver lining, they say. My sinuses were so bad that I carried a box of Kleenex around with me at school, and on hearing a question formulated that I couldn't answer, I just started blowing my nose to discourage the teacher from calling on me. It worked like a charm.

Only one change for the better had occurred since I was very young: I no longer became delirious every time my temperature went up. That phenomenon had given Anamary quite a rush when she first came to live with us, and there's no telling how less restrained people might have reacted had I continued casually hallucinating for what, to them, appeared to be no reason at all.

The "faith healers" occasionally found in the backwoods of Southeast Missouri some years before were all dead by the time I needed them. There was one I always enjoyed hearing about. He was called simply "Old Whistling Bill," and one of his notable talents was removing warts. Mother's hands once became so covered with them when she was young that she wore gloves to avoid embarrassment. Claud insisted on taking her to Bill, who, whistling all the while, looked at her hands and then observed that she must not have been keeping them very clean. Very funny. He rubbed the warts lightly and told her to go home and forget about them. She did.

A couple of weeks later, she was washing dishes and happened to think of her warts. She looked at her hands. The warts were all gone, completely and utterly. Some people might say that warts go away by themselves naturally if left to their own devices, but having had several "burned off" with liquid nitrogen—that came right back—I'm here to say that I would have greatly preferred someone to whistle mine off for good. In light of Anamary's *modus operandi*, I was not surprised to read in Colin Wilson's *Beyond the Occult* that "wart charmers whose 'charms' worked . . . simply repeated a text from the Bible which had been passed on to them by another wart-charmer." Unfortunately, he doesn't reveal what it was.

My uncle Marvin did locate a man in Poplar Bluff who was supposed to have some healing energy, so Anamary and I accompanied him there for a "reading." He correctly pinpointed the affected area of my body and gave me some "prayer rags" (little scraps of cloth) along with instruction for their use, but I had some trouble maintaining a properly reverent frame of mind when I attempted to implement their influence on Divine Will. I finally decided if God wouldn't cure me without them, there was small chance of His curing me with them, so I threw them away. So there it is. I got sicker.

One day a new dimension was added to the familiar onset of acute illness: severe chest pain. Since my doctor was out of town, Mother took me to a younger one whose shingle was still tacky to the touch. He listened to my lungs, nodded knowingly at the recitation of my progressive symptoms, and correctly diagnosed the problem, adding that surgery might help and recommending only two hospitals in the country where it was being done: Mayo Clinic and Barnes. The latter was much closer, so it was the logical choice.

It is incredible that medicine could have come so far just in the last half of the Twentieth Century. By comparison with present standards, procedures I underwent in the summer of 1949 were so primitive as to seem like relics of the medieval torture chamber. In fact, I'm sure that's where they originated.

Scratch any blessing on God's green earth, and you find a curse—and vice versa. Perhaps the Mexican artist Orozco had that in mind when he did his remarkable mural of God as a grinning, wild-eyed old man with schizophrenia written all over his face. At any rate, plastic is one of those dual-natured substances that in its more positive persona has been a major factor in revolutionizing medical technology. A diagnostic tool of pulmonary specialists was and still is the bronchoscope, a long, hollow device inserted into the bronchial tube and its branches for having a look or suctioning out extraneous matter. In 1949, this instrument was made of steel, ribbed for flexibility, and it was shoved into the mouth and down the throat with no benefit of anesthesia save for a token spray applied topically with the tongue grasped firmly and pulled out as far as it would come. The patient lay flat on his back blindfolded and looked to the Lord to be dismissed momentarily, for the infernal thing cut off all access to air and precluded even of grunt of protest.

The resident particularly charged with my care was Dr. John Bassett, and wherever he is today, there too is a sizable piece of my heart. He stood beside me during my first bronchoscopy (called, aptly enough, "swallowing the sword")—one of several strong men required to hold me down on the gurney in spite of the leather straps that bound me fast across the chest. Someone else, whom I suspected of wearing a black hood over his head, wielded the instrument of doom. Every time I was certain this was it, that I'd die if I couldn't take a breath, I gave Bassett's arm an horrendous pinch. The next day (I lived), he came to my room and silently rolled up a sleeve. The arm he extended for my inspection was covered with dark purple bruises—pinch-shaped. I felt awful and apologized profusely (in a hoarse whisper). He laughed and said that was okay, that he'd had worse. He had once been holding a man's hand when the patient went under the anesthesia. It turned out to be a virtual death grip from which he couldn't extricate himself, and as a consequence his own hand was useless for quite some time following the fellow's return to consciousness.

The bronchogram was lots of fun too, but it came nowhere close to the delights of a bronchoscopy. Warm, opaque oil is sprayed into the lungs, where it collects in any unnatural declivities caused by scar tissue or chronic infection, revealing them on X-ray film. One is forbidden to cough during this ordeal. Graham added a little excitement to it in the way of a tilting examination table that all but stood the patient on his head. An aide (Annie, an Afro-American who *really* ran the Chest Service) held on to one's ankles to prevent incidental skull fracture.

Having thus confirmed the hometown physician's diagnosis, the experts at Barnes decided that before lung surgery, I must have my sinuses reamed out. That process was also a lulu. Sitting bolt upright, conscious and blindfolded (again!), I played a live Galatea to Dr. Joseph Ogura's Pygmalion. Using a hammer (as in carpenter's tool), he literally chiseled through the bone over my upper gums on both sides, opened up the sinus cavities and drained them. Every blow on that chisel felt as if it were taking off the top of my head. It's not difficult to understand why all these folks were big on blindfolds! What kind of fool would hang around for treatment like that if he saw what was coming at him! I won't describe what happened to my nose, but to this day, its inner configuration elicits interesting murmurs from any doctor probing it.

When I was all trussed up with catgut and ready to return to my room, I must still have looked pretty gross, for the old Negro orderly sent to wheel me back was visibly outraged.

"I'm not takin' you to yo' mamma lookin' like that!" he snorted and proceeded to mop the blood off my face and neck himself and fetch me a clean gown. There undoubtedly weren't many malpractice suits back in those days—or maybe giving mothers heart attacks doesn't come under the rubric of malpractice. Actually, it smacks more of involuntary manslaughter. In the days to come, a couple of Black orderlies made it their particular mission to keep me amused, sometimes playing checkers with me. Every time one of them came into my room, I grabbed my cheeks in both hands and started begging, "Please don't make me laugh! Please don't make me laugh!"

In the years that have followed my encounter with Ogura, younger physicians have all but salaamed when I've mentioned his name. Apparently my claim to fame will rest on having been under his talented hammer.

I went home still looking like a gluttonous chipmunk to convalesce sufficiently for the really heavy stuff. A month later, we were back at Barnes, and I was gearing up for removal of the lower lobe of my right lung. Even after all I had gone through, I had no idea of what to expect, so I asked a woman who had already experienced the same surgery if it hurt much—any normal child's major concern. She looked at me rather disdainfully, I thought, and retorted, somewhat shortly, "Does it hurt to cut your finger?" Maybe she believed that's the only frame of reference a fourteen-year-old has for measuring pain, but then what else could she have said? Pain cannot be imagined. It can only be felt.

A week or so before I had returned to Barnes, an article appeared in the newspaper describing a medical first: a young man had suffered cardiac arrest during an operation, and the surgical team succeeded in starting his heart up again. He had come back from what was considered in those days to be "the dead." That's an intriguing term, by the way. It isn't "back from *death*"; it's back from *being with those who are dead*—an idiomatic bow to recognition of survival of the spirit, since no one suggests that the survivor joined others under the ground. Mother scoffed at the article and said that wasn't possible, attributing its claim to typical journalistic hyperbole. Whoever listens in on our little jests and reckless opinions must have said, "Oh, really?" For on August 9, 1949, that is exactly what happened to me.

Intensive care units and sophisticated life-support systems still belonged in the realm of science fiction, unfortunately. The report given my parents while I was still in the recovery room having a touch-and-go battle went roughly like this: Graham was carving away on me when one of his assistants said, "Oh, Doctor! Her heart's stopped beating!" The old surgeon instantly dropped his scalpel, plunged his hand into my open chest cavity, grabbed my heart firmly and began squeezing it rhythmically. He continued pumping it in this manner until it eventually began working on its own once more, albeit feebly. In the meantime, a heart specialist was paged and arrived with all due dispatch.

When I was first conscious of being back in my room, people moved about me like characters from a black and white movie. I could make them out, but they were colorless and difficult to see in the pervasive gloom. I had no concept of the passage of time, but my perception must have remained that way for a couple of days. I was in an old-fashioned oxygen tent that enveloped me like a cocoon of palpable, inescapable, incomprehensible pain. I couldn't move my right arm—not that I much cared to—nor turn myself over. Someone kept making an unreasonable demand that I cough, as if merely breathing weren't difficult enough. I tried, and the pain became hot daggers plunging into my right lung and twisting their way out. Dr. Bassett was there, trying to be funny. I smiled and whispered something about his not being a very good doctor, for he had almost lost me back there in the OR. He wheeled on my mother, who had turned away to stare vacantly out the window. She had just abandoned her imposed task of cleaning the clear polish off my nails because, as she told me later, they looked too much like a dead person's.

"Why did you do that!" he demanded to know. "Why did you tell this child what happened to her! You had no right to do that!"

His voice was unsteady. I have never seen anyone else as angry as he was at that moment.

Mother shook her head and said quietly, "I didn't tell her anything."

Nor, indeed, had anybody. With a weak gesture, I summoned Bassett closer.

"She's telling you the truth," I whispered. "I heard all of you talking about it when it happened."

And I had. I remembered watching them, standing there in the bright lights of the operating arena. I saw someone leave to page the cardiologist and saw him come in. I could have picked him out of any crowd. My "vision" was clear then and natural, not obscured as it was after I regained consciousness. One of the team had said, "It's no use," but someone else protested, "We can't give up, she has to live." It had been Dr. Bassett, who now stood looking at me with something akin to awe. Neither he nor Mother said anything—to me or to each other. After a long moment of silence, he turned and left the room, and the incident was not mentioned again. There was genuine concern that I might have suffered some brain damage, and one of my earliest impressions upon becoming conscious was of someone pulling a succession of toes and making me identify which was which. Apparently I got them all right.

It would be many years before Elizabeth Kübler-Ross would arrive on the scene to describe innumerable experiences of a similar nature. All Mother understood at the time was what another resident told her when it appeared that the scales had finally been tipped in favor of my surviving.

"It isn't anything we did," he said humbly. "Never before have I seen anyone fight for life unconsciously like this child did. The credit is hers, not ours."

Maybe I was just being my usual stubborn self. Maybe anything. But there was no "maybe" about the fact that my disembodied spirit had stood back and dispassionately eavesdropped on a frantic conversation regarding what to do about an uncooperative ticker in a chest gaping wide open at that very minute. Notified of my critical condition, relatives came to St. Louis from Dexter, stopping to pick up Anamary on the way. I had never addressed my uncles or aunts by those titles, yet when Marvin's face loomed before me, I said faintly, "Uncle Marvin! I didn't think I'd ever see you again!" His response was jocular, but I was told later that he then went out into the hall and wept like a baby.

I worshipped Dr. Graham, but I loved John Bassett. His Irish humor kept me going when that effort hardly seemed worthwhile. On the day I was scheduled to have my stitches removed, he sat out in the hallway at the nurses' station telling someone (or perhaps nobody) in a very loud voice what awful things were shortly in store for the patient in room such-and-such (mine). They made a bronchoscopy sound like a walk in the park. His litany of horrors ended with a reminder that the only escape available to the doomed victim was jumping out of a fifth-floor window. Then came a sinister laugh.

But he had obviously forgotten that a door joined the adjacent room to mine. I knew it was unoccupied, so I quietly slipped out of bed, went next door and hid. When he came in with his assistant in tow, I was nowhere to be found.

When he finally located me, I was marched back to bed and unstitched. Talking to the nurse beside him instead of me the whole time, he told her to remember someday when she read a book by Dorris June Brannon to recall that they had known that person when she had more lungs than she did now. He was cutting three-inch-wide tape and applying it liberally to the dressing that extended from my solar plexus all the way around under my right arm and up between my shoulder blades. With great solemnity, he spoke of this and that having nothing to do with me, as if he were scarcely aware that I was anywhere about. Cutting a piece of adhesive about six inches long, he then said to her, "You know, there's just one thing wrong with this hospital. It's too noisy. Therefore, I'm going to do something about it." With that, he slapped the tape over my mouth, patted it down firmly and walked out.

Several years later, I came under the care of Dr. Charles P. McGinty, who had also been a resident in Chest Service during the summer of 1949. He had doubtless been one of the many who trooped by on rounds every morning to regard me with the same curiosity people display towards caged animals in zoos. Charlie told me a delightful story about Bassett that bears preservation. Dr. Graham, according to McGinty, was a very "gross" surgeon—that is, he didn't subscribe to the practice of tying off little "bleeders" (small arteries). One day Dr. Bassett was assisting him and tied one off. Graham thundered, "I told you not to tie off an artery unless it has a name!"

With manly poise, the young resident gravely replied, "Sir, that's Artery Bassett." From then on, that became the moniker for all the little bleeders.

I was sent home with instructions that I should be brought back the following summer for surgery on the left lung. Something to look forward to. We did go back, and I was run through the paces again, but there was no surgery that time. Dr. Graham told *me* I was fine and could do anything I wanted now—swim (ha!), play tennis, toot my trombone if I must, anything in the wide world I felt like doing. He told my *parents*, however, that if he removed any more diseased tissue, I wouldn't have enough healthy lung left to sustain life. He added that the only way to prolong that life much longer was to keep me happy. Sure. No problem at all.

I missed school during all of September my sophomore year, but a couple of loyal friends came to my house regularly to keep me abreast of assignments—Nancy Cracraft in Spanish, and Rodney O'Connor in geometry. I had to walk with a crutch for some time to pull my right shoulder back up to its normal position, but I still occasionally went over to the football field first thing in the morning to sit in the bleachers and watch the marching band practice. I often cried. The late Leroy Mason, incidentally, was one of the finest directors ever to come down the pike. It was he who first hit upon the idea of having his band form letters and designs while playing at halftimes. He got the notion from watching lights on a store marquee spelling out an advertisement.

From Jackson High School, the art spread all over Missouri and, later, all over the country. When Mason eventually went from Jackson High to Southeast Missouri State University in Cape Girardeau, he put the Golden Eagles on the map and drew students from far and wide whose ambition was merely to play an instrument in his band. He was a perfectionist and a disciplinarian of military caliber. I can still see him atop the stadium shouting through his megaphone at some hapless component of the human configuration sprawled across the yard lines. "There's a hole there I could drive my car through!" entered our vernacular as a designation for any inappropriate gap, whether in logic or the seat of somebody's pants.

My cough was as productive as ever, but at least the chills and fever abated. No more than I knew about good health, that seemed tantamount to being well. The resulting *joie de vivre* led to a setback, however, from which I never fully returned to immediate post-surgical status. The following winter, on a walk in the country, I broke through the ice on a creek I was crossing and all but froze my feet. By the time I reached my uncle's house, my chest was already getting congested, and I lapsed into one of my old bouts of severe bronchitis. I was still able to eat hamburgers again, though, since part of the locus of my virulent chronic infection had been removed.

Because I now had a terminal case of hero worship, I disregarded all my native talents and determined to become a doctor and pass on to others the miracle of life that Graham had given me. That was a mistake—the only evidence that perhaps I had suffered some oxygen-deficit brain damage after all. My grades and extracurricular activities got me into college on a modest National Honor Society scholarship. There I learned to my sorrow that physicians are more than humanitarian healers: they must demonstrate a considerable flair for such things as physics and organic chemistry. Alas. By my junior year, I was a music major (piano), but then I became acutely ill again and was told never to go back to school and never to work. That left one option, and I took it. As luck would have it, I didn't display much aptitude for marriage either.

CHAPTER NINE

All my young life—Anamary notwithstanding—I longed for a brother or sister, preferably the former. Sometimes I made up an older sibling who was away at school and even convinced my playmates that this was the gospel truth. I adored the infants who crossed my path and contrived, unsuccessfully, to keep one or two. A family acquaintance once left her six-month-old son with us while she stayed with her husband at the hospital. He was dying of cancer. We had little Bobby for many weeks. When his father finally passed away and his mother came back to get him, I threw a double conniption.

Screaming and crying, I yelled at her, "You can't have him! He's our baby!"

He wasn't, and she took him home, only to let him die of pneumonia a few months later. She had rubbed goose grease on his chest by way of treatment. I never forgave her.

I did succeed in snagging Bette's new kitten once and "helped" her look for it high, low and in between when she came inquiring after it. I had waited patiently until it wandered across the property line and then applied the nine points of common law having to do with possession. Long after Bette returned home empty-handed, Mother found the cat asleep in the middle of her bed. She was not amused and was even less entertained by the use to which it had put the throw rug beside the bed. My petty theft on this occasion was merely a secondary source of her distress. It was not overlooked, however, in the general excitement.

I meddled a good deal, I must admit, and was still at it when I blundered upon my original birth certificate while rummaging through Dad's desk one day when I was eleven. For the first time,

I saw my biological mother's name. The effect was similar to that experienced by the person who innocently takes hold of an electric fence: I had an impulse to turn the thing loose, but I couldn't. It suddenly converted fantasy to a real person with an actual identity. That meant she also had actual dimensions and other interesting features that I grudgingly conceded might not correspond to the portrait I had created for her in my mind's eye.

The need to investigate further got the better of my desire to avoid reprisal for snooping. When I took the document to Mother, she didn't scold but told me all she herself knew, which wasn't much. It was enough to place my maternal grandparents geographically in Southeast Missouri and to characterize them by rumor as fine, God-fearing people. The telltale paper was returned to safekeeping in its drawer, and nothing else was said about the discovery. The certificate itself revealed that my birth mother was twenty-two when she had me and that she either didn't know my father's name or, more likely, protected his "honor" against public disgrace. The space provided for his identity was blank. From what I was able to piece together years later, I think she was paid to keep mum—not an unusual scenario for 1935 or any other year, for that matter.

When I was older, Mother saved newspaper clippings for me that contained reference to anyone with the distaff half of my family name: my grandmother's obituary, for example, and another when a second cousin died who had been a prominent doctor in Doniphan, Missouri. By then I was married and living in Tucson, Arizona, and on a whim, I sent a card of condolence to his father—my great uncle—whose little grocery store I had chanced upon in Dexter one time quite by accident. Much to my surprise, his wife—the doctor's stepmother—responded. Here was a golden opportunity to find out what had become of "Ms. Dee", we'll call her for the sake of confidentiality. I wrote back and casually asked where she lived at the time, as if I had lost track of an old acquaintance. The ruse worked, but I learned much more than I had bargained for. She lived, answered my informant, in Michigan *near her daughter!*

I had not factored a sister into my fantasies, and I was numb with shock. Was I a twin? Surely Dr. Annie would not have split us up. Had Ms. Dee married, and were there other children besides? Questions representing a jumble of possibilities whirled through my head. To think that I had spent all those frustrating years as an only child when somewhere I had a sibling gave rise to a resentment entirely foreign to my experience and even to my nature. I could forgive Ms. Dee for adopting me out, but not for depriving me of the joy, the solace, the company, the friendship that, by example, Mother and Anamary had proved were available to sisters. The urge to locate mine, to rush immediately into her arms, was almost more than I could resist. I wrote back to my voluble correspondent requesting more specific details.

This time she smelled a rat, as the saying goes, and put some specific questions back to me by way of reply, adding the name and address of one of my aunts, who she said could be of more help. I lost no time in following up on her lead and thus began corresponding with one of Ms. Dee's sisters. Ms. Dee, I learned, was the youngest of the family and something of a maverick who had all but completely severed her ties with her relatives shortly after I was born. "Aunt Jo," a name which will sufficiently protect her anonymity, invited me to visit her, and when I did, she had no trouble at all accepting our kinship as fact. I bore so striking a resemblance to my grandmother and to another aunt who was also deceased that I could have passed for the ghost of either.

People who take family resemblances for granted cannot imagine the sense of awe and delight that swept over me the first time I saw my maternal grandmother's photograph. After twenty-six years of not looking like anybody and then beholding a face that mine would, in all probability, exactly replicate in another fifty literally took my breath away. It was as if I had found myself for the first time, fixed in both the past and future at the selfsame instant. That, of course, is the essence of heritage—a point on a continuum.

Those who aren't adopted themselves cannot comprehend how it feels to be without that *place*, that *reason* for being one way and not another. To be adopted is to be born in the middle of a novel without beginning or end. It is to weigh anchor on a real enough ship, but one that sails forever in a boundless void.

Ms. Dee apparently had a considerable reputation for being disagreeable, for Aunt Jo wanted no occasion to tangle with her. She therefore refused even to drive me by my sister's house on the outside chance that our mutual mother might be there, recognize the car, and suspect some mischief. I was not eager to lock horns with her either. I'd had a mother and felt no irresistible urge to meet another one. I was further put off by the fact that she had attended her mother's funeral and taken pictures of the corpse, although she hadn't bothered to visit the lady while she was still alive for a total of ten years.

I did, however, keep a promise to myself of very long standing: I wrote her an anonymous letter without a return address, identifying who I was by circumstance so that there could be no doubt as to when and where our paths had crossed. With it I discharged what I considered to be my only obligation to her—to let her know that I was alive and had been loved and cared for very well indeed. I enclosed a photo, for it seemed to me a woman could never help wondering how her child turned out as an adult. She worked at the same factory where Aunt Jo's husband was employed. Apparently she did receive the letter and put two and two together correctly, for she descended on him with both feet about Jo's nosing into her affairs and made it very plain that her married daughter, along with her daughter's children, was the only family she had. Period.

Because Ms. Dee and her other daughter were very close, I realized I could not in good conscience reveal myself to the latter and risk interfering with, if not destroying, their relationship. It was a bitter sacrifice. I had learned that my sister was two years old than I; that she too had been "illegitimate," although the identity of her father was well known, and that she had been left in her grandparents' care while her mother worked several miles away in Poplar Bluff, sending money home for her support. One aunt I was to meet later had been aware that Ms. Dee was pregnant a second time, but she was told that the baby died at birth. A fitting enough report for a life that was to be a kind of farcical *danse de Macabre.*

There was nothing to do but wait, and I did—for twenty years. Sometimes during that long interval, I toyed with several ideas for at least seeing my sister face to face. One was to pose as an Avon Lady. Another was to pretend I was conducting a survey of some kind. The fear of being recognized as a relative of some sort prevailed, though, and I never carried out any of my clever schemes. I kept in sporadic touch with Aunt Jo, a warm and gracious person, and let sleeping dogs lie

Then one day Aunt Jo called to say Ms. Dee had died (at sixty-four of cancer). If I still wanted to contact my sister, she felt I was now free to do so. She gave me a name and a town and wished me luck.

I began my search through Ma Bell with the kind cooperation of an operator who provided all the listings of that surname along with addresses and telephone numbers. To avoid being taken for some sort of kooky crank and hung up on, I elected to introduce myself through the U.S. Mail. One after another, my letters came back stamped "Addressee unknown." It finally dawned on me that my aunt had provided erroneous information. I was sure, however, of Ms. Dee's married name, so I hit upon the notion of phoning all the funeral homes in the town where she had lived. Bingo. The first one I called had conducted her funeral, and on merely being told that I was a relative who wanted to get in touch with her daughter, the lady on the other end of the line gave me her name, address and *unlisted* number without the slightest hesitation, volunteering that she knew the family well (small wonder, as it turned out), and that it included three "very lovely daughters." By then I had three sons, a complementary happenstance to say the least.

The letter I set about composing was the most difficult to construct of any I have ever written. It required a careful inventory of my assets and liabilities, a cautious weeding out of anything that might offend or intimidate. How thick *is* blood compared to water? What if she were my opposite in all matters political and philosophical? Would she even like me as a person, let alone as a sister? Would I like her? I was forty-three, and she was forty-five. After all that time, would she be able to let me into her life? The questions were endless and the answers inaccessible. I did the best I could and enclosed photographs and a copy of that fateful birth certificate bearing our mother's signature.

Weeks passed and then months. There was no reply, but the letter was not returned. When the Christmas holidays approached, I sent her a card. There was only silence, deep as God's or a winter evening's. Assuming that she could not handle the sudden trauma of my disclosure, I gave up further attempts to contact her. Rejection should have been old hat by then, but this one hurt.

Two years went by. I was commuting a hundred and thirty miles to Washington University in St. Louis as a graduate student two or three times weekly. One cold January night I came home to find a letter I had quit expecting. With trembling fingers, I tore it open. There was no explanation for the long delay, nor was there encouragement to pursue to any logical conclusion the overtures I had made.

"I don't blame you for trying to find your family," she wrote, "but I don't think I'm part of it."

She did go on to ask, however, if I had approached her aunts with the information I had sent her. I fired a letter back, affirming that I had and reasserting the validity of my claim on her kinship. I suggested that she call me on the following Sunday, which, by a happy coincidence, would be my forty-fifth birthday.

I hadn't been up long on the appointed day when the phone rang. Fearing to hope, I answered it. An unfamiliar but very nice female voice asked, "Is this June?"

Tears ran down my face.

"Yes, and you're Katie," I replied. "It's snowing here. What's it doing there?"

Thank whatever gods may be for the mundane when the extraordinary threatens to sweep us away in a deluge of our own emotions. I clung to those snowflakes like a drowning man to straws. They were individually and collectively the most important things in the world right at that moment, and the most beautiful. When we had exhausted all possible comparisons of local weather conditions respectively, it seemed safe enough to hazard more relevant topics. Katie invited me to come visit her, and a date was set in March that would be convenient for both of us.

What a waste our agonies often turn out to be. While I had brooded over her failure to respond, Katie had searched in vain for my first letter, which had just seemed to disappear into thin air. My Christmas card, she said, bore no return address and no last name. The missing correspondence did not surface until a married daughter removed some of her belongings from her mother's to her own home in preparation for another daughter's wedding. When unpacking some boxes, she discovered the letter and called her mother immediately. It was then that Katie had written her skeptical reply.

During the interim, she had lost her oldest daughter and her only son, the former to complications attendant upon retardation resulting from concurrent cases of measles and chicken pox in early childhood and the latter from a terrible car wreck. It would not have been a propitious time for my intrusion into her world. As it was, she could still doubt my authenticity and deal with death unhindered by the additional heavy burden of, in a sense, losing her mother all over again, for that is the effect my existence had for her. The person she thought she knew better than anyone else had really been a stranger, a kind of living lie who had concealed a vital part of her past.

It had not been a comfortable lie. Incredulous, Katie recalled how upset her mother had become every time she heard that someone let a child out for adoption. "They just give them away like little puppy dogs!" she would exclaim with vehemence. How well she knew! For some time before she died, she also frequently hallucinated a young woman with dark hair, quite possibly a reconstruction of the photograph I had sent her so long before. Katie said she would frequently ask, "Who is that dark-haired girl there [with one or the other of her granddaughters]?" Katie, rather than try to explain, would pass the apparition off as a friend.

My own life had taken several ninety-degree turns in the twenty years I had waited to make myself known to my sister: the birth of my first son, divorce, return to Missouri, a second marriage and two additional children, the death of my father at 74—the list would grow tedious. Mother and Anamary had become so advanced in age that they could no longer take care of a house properly, so Mother and I both sold our homes and pooled the income from them to build a place in the country where "the girls," as they were known to my husband and me, would have a suite of their own, be as independent as they like, but live in the bosom of a family to love and care for them whenever that became necessary. They were overjoyed at the prospect of my meeting Katie and sincerely hoped that the new relationship would flourish and become a source of comfort to me when I no longer had them in my life. There wasn't a shred of jealousy or possessiveness in their hearts.

Time dragged like a sled on thick mud, but March came anyway. At last I was on a plane bound for Michigan, my heart pounding and my palms sweaty. By fits and turns, I was seized by a nearly hysterical urge to laugh and cry simultaneously. What does one say to a sister she has never met? "Hi, there"? Katie had said I could recognize her by locating a small boy with red hair, for her daughter and son-in-law and their child would be with her.

I entered the terminal wearing sunglasses to hide my blurry eyes and began searching faces for one I expected somehow to strike a familiar chord in my soul. None did, and I saw no red-haired child. Perhaps Katie had chickened out at the last minute. I stood there alone and perplexed in a crowd of happy, reuniting people. Then off to the side I spotted them, watching and waiting at a distance.

"Are you looking for me by any chance?" I asked, walking up to the little group.

It seemed natural to be there, to embrace the woman who held out her arms. There was a comfortable feel about them, like the feel of old friends picking up where they left off back in high school or college. There had been a hiatus, that's all.

What a contrast we made, Katie and I—she with her blue-eyed fairness and short stature and I with my brown eyes, dark hair and greater height. I loved her laugh immediately and knew it came from a good heart and a generous nature. We gingerly explored tangential issues. We were of the same political party and shared the same attitudes towards pressing social concerns of the day. Her mind was keen and her wit quick—qualities I particularly value. We both possessed a mystical bent and had been drawn to the occult to varying degrees, as had our mutual mother.

The differences were complementary rather than divisive. I was aggressive, she rather passive. As we traded tales from our separate childhoods, she laughed and observed that I would probably have gotten her into a lot of trouble, for she—although older—would have followed my lead. She had no creative talent of which she was aware, but there was an aura of stability about her that I lacked.

We spent three days catching up on a lifetime. Katie took me to visit the graves of her mother and of her son and daughter. Sadly enough, the tree into which her son's car had crashed stood directly opposite the entrance to the cemetery. It must have been a terrible effort for her to pass by it. There was snow on the ground, and I brushed it off Ms. Dee's headstone to read the epitaph. I had a strange paucity of any emotion whatsoever other than to feel slightly like an interloper. I wondered whether she would have wanted me to be standing there with Katie in violation of the secrecy she had so carefully preserved. Was she aware now, I mused, of the irony implicit in having abandoned the child so much more like her than the one she kept. My middle niece had gasped, "Look there, Mom!" as we were sitting at the table one day. She pointed to a dark mole on the top of my right hand. Ms. Dee had also had just such a mole in precisely the same spot on her own right hand. I had her coloring and eyes too, and even her expression. And certainly her temper.

I exulted in the process of discovery that continued during my visit and rejoiced in the manifold delightful surprises that emerged from it, but all the while, a part of me nagged more and more insistently, "I want to go home! I want to go home!" When I did go, having extracted from Katie a promise to return the visit, my husband picked me up at the airport and drove me to his office, where we had previously agreed to wait until the boys got out of school. We were then to pick them up and go out to dinner. I had scarcely settled into a chair when I began to cry—great sobs that racked my whole body. A dam burst inside my very soul, and a purgation long overdue emptied it of forty-five years' worth of accumulated garbage. As soon as I could talk, I said, "You'll just have to wait for me. I'm going home."

The twenty-five-mile drive seemed to take twice as long as usual. When I pulled up to the house, Mother and Anamary were sitting in front of the kitchen window they loved so much. I got out of the car and ran inside. Tears streaming, I went to Mother first and threw my arms around her, exclaiming, "I'm so glad you were my mother!" Embracing Anamary next, I told her, "I'm so glad you were my Anamary!" I was ready then to go back and proceed with the evening's agenda.

Of all the things I've had to be grateful for, I am most grateful that these two very special women lived long enough to hear me say, in effect, that had I been given a choice, I would have chosen them and the kind of life they made possible for me over any others in the wide world. It was only by comparison that I had finally come to grasp the breadth of my experience and the richness of the heritage that was as much mine as if I had been born to it. I learned that, in a very real way, the *fortunate* adopted child is greater than the sum of his parts as a result of the diversity of influences brought to bear upon the finished product.

The Jonathan apple grafted onto a Golden Delicious tree must sometime know more about Jonathans, however, than what he is able to extrapolate from his limited impression of self in order to be comfortable with his uniqueness. Nourished by his host's sap, he can be as healthy as environmental characteristic permit, but to feel at home among his yellow companions, he must also know how other Jonathans look and why he is different from the apples around him.

CHAPTER TEN

If I was "strange," as the Rev. Leona Boyles observed, I came by it honestly. Katie recounted how her mother had gone to a hypnotist and learned how to put herself into a trance. While she was in that state, Katie would read the racing forms to her, and she would pick out winning horses. Once she was vacationing in a cabin in Northern Michigan and called her daughter, requesting that she find out if a horse was running that anything to do with a red bird in its name. Katie looked. There was a Cardinal running. Ms. Dee said, "Put money on it." Katie did, and it came in first. The two of them raked in quite a bit before they began listening to men in the family who subscribed to other methods of gambling.

Katie herself learned how to tell fortunes with a regular deck of playing cards. Sometimes she did it just for a lark to entertain her children's friends. On one such occasion, her son George insisted that she do a reading for him too. She looked at the spread laid on the table at his request and blurted out, "You'll be dead a week from today." Everyone laughed. Exactly a week later he was driving home from work in a rainstorm, skidded into a tree and was killed. Nobody laughed. It was also exactly a year from the day his grandmother had died.

People who consider clairvoyance evil imagine somehow that the prediction itself causes the occurrence. This is unadulterated nonsense. If it worked that way, we'd all go around predicting whatever we choose to have happen. We would also have only to predict our enemies' demise, and we'd be rid of them. That is, if they didn't predict ours first. To ascribe some sinister power to clairvoyants also denies omnipotence to a deity theoretically in control of the whole show. But is that theory seriously entertained? I wonder.

My own dalliance with the occult took a slightly different tack from Katie's and her mother's. I read a book by Ruth Montgomery once and decided if she could do "automatic writing," so could I. After a few trial runs when my pen made circles and doodles, I began to get words and sentences. It was, and is, and interesting phenomenon about which I have yet to arrive at any definite conclusions. Over the years, "The Writing" has been uncannily accurate about some things and miserably inaccurate regarding others. Once a friend asked me to inquire of it whether the man she was dating would propose. The answer scribbled back said that he would do so before the summer was up (he did), and it gratuitously added that her recently married son—happily so to all appearances—would be divorced within two years (he was).

In response to a telephone query, it one time located a lost necklace fifty miles away in a house I had never seen. Its real forte was spells for various purposes (which I never had the nerve to use) and profound bits of personal advice. The most notable came in answer to a question about how to enhance attractiveness. I quote verbatim: "When you look in the mirror each day to wash or apply makeup, say to yourself, 'May the beauty of my spirit shine in my face for all to see so that I may be loved as my soul deserves.'" Those who are conscious of the fact that true beauty does come from within and who deliberately strive for it there will always present a more comely mien than those who think beauty is "only skin deep."

There is another useful suggestion from The Writing that I heartily recommend. It, too, concerns appearance. There is no better a skin toner than a simple solution it offered: "Place the rind of three lemons in three cups of cold water. Bring to a boil and boil three minutes. Let cool. Strain into an earthenware jar and keep in a cool place. Apply to the face on a cotton ball two or three times a day." This inexpensive remedy will heal minor lesions and skin abrasions that medicinal preparations fail to relieve. Apparently there is a crucial balance between the astringency of the citric acid and the rind's essential oil. Anamary once developed a lesion on her nose that would scab over and flake off, only to scab over again. Even cortisone cream proved ineffective in treating it. I finally got her to try the lemon-rind "cure" several times a day. The place healed perfectly in no time at all and remained normal when applications were discontinued.

Whether The Writing comes from within or from some independent entity—or a combination of both—I leave for others to speculate upon, but I would seriously hope that some of the bizarre things I have experienced over the years were not of *my* doing, consciously or unconsciously!

For example, I once asked my oldest son for the use of his car on the following Sunday to drive a friend some distance away for the purpose of investigating business prospects in West Virginia. Though usually more than willing to comply with such a request, he refused that time. The reason given was that he did not want to be a party to my friend's moving away from the religious community of which he thought she ought to remain a part (but to which she herself felt no commitment).

On that very Sunday morning, he was driving back from services, skidded on barely wet pavement, ran broadside into another car and totaled his own. Fortunately, he was not hurt, aside from banging his knee a bit. I certainly had no ill will towards him or his automobile, but the first thing I thought of on hearing about the accident was the fact that it wouldn't have occurred had he not exhibited so narrow an opinion of what was appropriate and thwarted my earnest desire to help someone in need. It made me recall other instances when, in retrospect, it seemed that some force beyond my control actively intervened in my affairs, often on my behalf, without being asked to.

About a year before that, while I was still living in Oregon the first time, my youngest son, Danny, received a plane ticket from his father for his semiannual trip to California to visit. We both looked at it, as did Charles, his older brother who was living at home again. On the day of Danny's scheduled departure, Charles had been using the car and was bringing it back some half-hour before time to leave for the airport about fifty miles away when the water hose burst. He assured me he still had time to buy another and install it, so he went to pick one up at an auto-parts store.

While he was still gone, a friend of Danny's who had stopped by to see him off asked what time his flight was supposed to leave. We told him. At that point, Danny handed him the ticket. Imagine our dismay and chagrin to learn, on his examination of it, that Danny should have been in Portland boarding the plane at that very minute! I called the airline's ticketing agent and explained that we were having car trouble, not mentioning our collective stupidity. She said the ticket would still be honored on the next available flight—at six o'clock the next morning—if we came on to the airport as soon as possible to take care of the change.

Charles returned and made the necessary repairs, and Danny and I drove to Portland as instructed. On the way there, it suddenly occurred to me that had all three of us not made the same error regarding the original flight time, the water hose would have burst about halfway to the airport, not only causing Danny to miss his plane, but leaving us stranded with a disabled vehicle and no money with which to have it towed or fixed en route. What had seemed initially to be a stroke of bad luck proved to be extremely good fortune. It was as if something had fed the same misinformation into all our minds quite deliberately.

An even more fantastic series of strangely "coincidental" events had occurred a few months prior to the water-hose episode. Though divorced, my third husband and I maintained a cordial relationship. I was about the only friend he could turn to when in the throes of his periodic bouts of psychosis, which were related to a tragic drug addiction. I first knew something was wrong that time when his employer called to say he had not shown up for work. Contrary to her expectations, I hadn't the vaguest clue as to where he might be.

Two days passed. Then I received a call from him. He was at a pay phone in Reno, and a taxi driver was waiting to be paid. Roberto had no money on him, although he had cashed a paycheck before leaving Oregon. He had no recollection of where he had left either his wallet or his car. I could tell from talking to him that he was psychotic again, so I asked to speak to the cabbie.

I told the fellow that he had a very sick man on his hands and that he should contact the Sheriff's office immediately and have them take his passenger to the nearest mental health facility. I said he could send me a bill for the fare that was due. As it turned out, he had already summoned the Highway Patrol regarding the fare, and he promised to pass on the information I had provided. I also requested that they phone me after getting Roberto admitted for psychiatric care.

Time went by, and I had no word. I tried each of the various law-enforcement agencies in Reno. All I could determine was that Roberto had not been incarcerated. Finally I obtained the number of the State Hospital and called there, but without much hope of getting any information. It is normally impossible even to determine whether a particular individual is a patient, much less be permitted to speak to him, without prior authorization from the patient himself, but I boldly asked for Roberto as if I didn't know any better. The receptionist at the central control office asked if he worked there. I replied, again rather boldly, that he was a patient. There was a brief pause, and she said, "Oh, yes. He's on such-and-such a ward." I heard a phone ringing. Against rather large odds, Roberto answered it himself.

I was in contact with his doctor and social worker during the next two weeks, in addition to speaking with Roberto fairly often. I had said I would be responsible for picking him up whenever he could be discharged. In the meantime, I needed desperately to find out what had happened to the missing wallet and the car, so I began calling casinos I knew Roberto favored when in Reno. The wallet was being held at one (with most of the paycheck cash still in it), and the car turned up in the garage of another. I identified myself to both of the casino representatives and explained the current dilemma. The one holding the wallet said he would cut a check for the amount of money it contained and mail it out to me.

I made the other fellow promise he would not turn the car keys over to anyone but me. I was thus able to pay Robert's rent and utility bills and assuage my fear of what might happen should he sign himself out of the hospital before he had sufficiently recovered to drive responsibly.

At the end of two weeks, the treating physician called to say Roberto would be discharged the next day. I was appalled. I knew the manifestations of his symptoms well enough to be reasonably sure he was still severely psychotic from having just talked to him that same day. I tried to dissuade the doctor from carrying out his decision, giving my reasons, but he was adamant in the position that unless observed by the staff in some overtly aberrant behavior, Roberto could not be legally held any longer. I almost refused to come get him, but then I asked the physician whether he would at least have the patient heavily sedated when I arrived to pick him up. Again the answer was no. That would be a breach of medical ethics.

I equivocated until I had spoken with Roberto's psychiatrist in Oregon and extracted from him a promise that a room would be waiting for him in Salem's general hospital the moment I returned from Nevada with him. I notified Reno I would be there the next morning and caught a bus.

During the subsequent long tiring night, I grappled with questions of what to do about the situation awaiting me. The only definite plan I had was to hide Roberto's keys (I had a set of my own) so that the chance of his getting control of the car and leaving me stranded someplace in the wilds of northern Nevada would be somewhat reduced.

On arriving in Reno, I took a cab to the casino where the car was still parked. To my boundless relief and delight, the garage attendant could not locate Roberto's keys anywhere. For all practical purposes, they had completely disappeared, and the supervisor, who might have had some information concerning their whereabouts, was off duty and couldn't be reached by phone. I wouldn't have to hide them or lie either.

When I walked into the State Hospital, the doctor greeted me with "We tried to reach you, but you had already left! I was going to tell you not to come!" Too late, he had discovered that my assessment of Roberto's condition was right after all. I was given the option of leaving him in Reno for an indefinite period, but after considering all the factors involved—not least of which was the inconvenience of getting there—I said I would take him back with me for further treatment at home. The doctor assured me they had sedated Roberto so heavily that he was "barely moving." At my request, he gladly provided me with additional medication to administer if necessary on the return trip. Worry number two was neatly eliminated. Roberto remained docile all the way back to Oregon—he had a history of violence when ill—and, because I had trusted my judgment, arrangements were in place for continuing his therapy immediately upon our arrival there. His car keys, by the way, never were found.

The sheer weight of this and much additional evidence that I had the protection of some agent prone to dispense swift retribution when I was wronged sometimes almost frightened me by its implications, grateful as I was—and am. I certainly don't flatter myself that I deserve such particular attention. Actually, it's probably something most of us enjoy without being conscious of the fact. Who can say how many near misses we all have with potential calamity that we never even become aware of?

Common enough in the annals of the occult but far from being universally experienced are clairvoyant dreams. I've had these from time to time—usually about nothing of consequence, however. A couple of notable exceptions are discussed in *Mostly Reliable Recollections*. The events dreamed commonly took place the following day and were sometimes no more momentous than receiving a letter whose contents were precisely those foretold in my sleep.

Once when I was about eight, a friend spent the night with me, and we both slept with Anamary. I dreamed a young woman with red hair appeared at the footboard and said, "I'm going to make your bed fall." I scarcely had time to remonstrate when the slats, springs and mattress under me and my companions suddenly dropped to the floor. The jolt dislodged coal stored in a bin directly below the bedroom, all of which combined to catapult Mother and Dad out of their bed, certain of an earthquake.

Dreams have always been highly respected as a source of knowledge and inspiration. As Cirlot states in *A Dictionary of Symbols*,

> . . . they afford Man another means of making contact with his deepest aspirations, with the geometric or moral laws of the universe, and also with the muted stirring of the submerged unconscious.

The Bible is replete with accounts of dreams as vehicles of Divine message. The Association for Research and Enlightenment, an organization arising from the mystical experience of Edgar Cayce, incorporates study into the genesis and meaning of dreams, and some psychologists and psychiatrists employ them almost exclusively as a diagnostic tool in their treatment modality. The latter approach, however, emphasizes symbolism pervaded by a materialistic tone rather than metaphysical, which is cosmic in scope.

Orthodox Jews still interpret sleep as being one-sixtieth part of death and bless God every morning for restoring souls to dead bodies. This reflects the belief that one's spirit walks abroad while one sleeps (a common notion in primitive societies) and would cover very nicely a dream Anamary had once.

I was still living in Tucson, and Mother and Dad had gone away for a few days to take care of something to do with his parents. Anamary reported that one night while they were gone, she dreamed she awoke to find me standing beside her bed. Astonished not so much that I was in Missouri as by her bed, she asked how I had gotten there.

"Oh, I got in all right," I replied.

She awoke, reflected on the dream a bit, went back to sleep and dreamed the same thing again. This process was repeated once more without variation. The next morning, she found the front door standing wide open.

One has to know the degree to which Anamary was obsessively compulsive about locking the doors at night to appreciate the full import of this sequence of events. It was she who always took care of that final preparation for retirement, and she did it with a certainly that allowed her no qualms about going to sleep with a full sense of safety. Had there been any doubt whatsoever in her mind as to the fastness of the front-door lock, she would have leapt out of bed following the first of the three identical dreams and checked the entire premises for breaches of security, especially since she was there alone.

There is a prayer in the *siddur* mentioned earlier having specifically to do with dreams, attributing them to God and requesting that good ones be fulfilled and bad ones be remedied, or "healed," to nullify their negative effect and change it to a positive one. Judging from the number of unfulfilled dreams I have had involving tragedy that I bent a considerable amount of will toward wishing to be averted, it might be well not to scoff too cynically at that ancient bow to the role of the unconscious in human affairs.

I am always particularly respectful of dreams whose setting is realistic—that is, an actual environment that exactly duplicates one in which the sleeper lives or with which he is intimately familiar. They stand a much better chance of representing a true paranormal experience. One that still haunts me occurred about four years after Anamary's death. I had moved twice since then and, being divorced, occupied a bedroom alone. Whether I really awoke or dreamed I awoke is moot, but for the sake of argument, we'll say I dreamed that I woke up and sensed a body in bed with me. The complication was that my "awakening" interrupted a totally different and somewhat bizarre dream in progress.

Although the drapes were closed, a streetlight just outside dispelled the darkness, and I could see well the open closet at the foot of my bed with my clothes hanging precisely as I had actually left them. I lay there frozen, scarcely able to breathe. What should I do: remain motionless and pretend I was really sleeping? Make a dash for the door? Die instantly? There just weren't a whole lot of acceptable alternatives. I took a mental inventory of handy weapons. Other than *Webster's Unabridged Dictionary* on a nearby shelf, there weren't any. Even if I could bash in a head with it, I'd wake the intended victim (assuming he or she was asleep) just heaving it over my own for leverage.

Fatalistically, I finally decided to see whose form was stretched out there alongside me, and with great effort of will, I turned my head and looked. It was Anamary! I had never been in the habit of swearing or using Anglo-Saxon words in general disfavor, but I blurted out, "Jesus Christ, Anamary! You scared the shit out of me!" At that, we both howled with laughter, and I turned over and went back to sleep—or dreamed I did—as if this had been a perfectly normal experience. I should have asked her how *she* got there!

Various methods for stimulating prophetic dreams have been bandied about for ages. An interesting one still in current use is very simple. If the problem or question involves another person of the opposite sex, his or her name is written nine times on a piece of paper. The name of the one seeking information or insight is written nine times on the other side. This is then rolled around nine bills of any denomination—ones, fives, tens, whatever—and tied with a ribbon. The bundle is placed under one's pillow and slept on every night until the desired dream is induced. This is an old Gypsy trick, and I tried it once with fascinating results, but like everything else of such a nature, there are never any guarantees of success.

I see no reason why this practice should be regarded as more "evil" than any of the modern scientific approaches to dream control. Mystical properties have been ascribed to certain numbers from antiquity, three and nine particularly. Indeed, Peter Tompkins, in *The Mystery of the Great Pyramid*, goes so far as to postulate that God might be, essentially, the value pi, which, as far as anyone has ever been able to determine, is infinite. It is no accident that letters in the Hebrew alphabet double as numbers. This conveys to every word a particular "energy," as it were, resulting in the occult system of numerology, which accounts for many practices among Jewish sects whose roots reach far back into the Oral Tradition, from which kabalistic works were distilled. During the Middle Ages, magic formulae were composed on this basis, among them *abracadabra*, derived from the Hebrew phrase *abrek ad habra*, meaning *It is created as I speak*.

The twenty-eight letters of the Arabic language, corresponding to the days in the lunar month, were also assigned numerical values. In fact, Cirlot states that

> Man, in every system ever formulated, has always tried to prove the divine power of letters by making them dependent upon mystic and cosmic orders.

The principal objection among the religious to employing unorthodox shortcuts to knowledge or manipulation of events is the belief that they somehow circumvent God's will or detract from the concept of His exclusively absolute power. If His power is absolute, it cannot be circumvented in the first place, yet prayer is little more than an attempt to manipulate the future. Its track record is no better than that of the best occult efforts when it comes to successful results. One always hears about it when prayer "heals" the mortally ill, but not much is said when the mortally ill die in spite of pious petitions to the Almighty. Failures are merely attributed to His will. Whatever that "will" represents is doubtless the bottom line anyway and would logically seem to be as much involved with the outcome in occult as well as in religious circles.

As far as that's concerned, do we not seek advice from lawyers, from doctors, from pastors, from counselors, from meteorologists who forecast the weather in an attempt not only to prepare ourselves for the future, but to alter its course for our greatest benefit? Does anyone but the most extreme fanatics on the fringes of modern civilization leave every facet of life to "the providence of God, who alone knows the future," as *The Catholic Encyclopedia* (1976 edition) puts it?

There is another troublesome discrepancy; it seems to me, in the almost frenetic interdiction found in the Judeo-Christian tradition against probing the future. If the "spirit of life" breathed exclusively into man and interpreted as that soul which is reflective of God and eternal ("Know ye not that ye are the temple of God?" asks Jesus) is indeed a spark of the Divine, then is it not probably imbued with at least minute traces of all that constitutes that original Essence, including prescience?

It is significant that for many centuries the Church denounced *science*—which basically means *knowledge*—as bitterly as it still denounces *pre*science, or *fore*knowledge. Science, we all know, deals as much with probability as with certainty, and its hypotheses, like all predictions, must ultimately be put to and stand the test of practical verification. To inquire of destiny no more violates the "providence of God" than to investigate the nature of an atom, for destiny merely defines what is *possible*. The outcome still depends upon the agency of free will. It may or may not be fulfilled. If one is not *destined*, for example, to become a doctor (as I obviously wasn't), no amount of ambition or study is going to bring that about. On the other hand, if the destiny is given, the individual still has to apply himself properly for it to be realized.

Except for Miriam, Deborah and Hulda, the biblical prophets are men. "Fortune-tellers,' however—dating back to the Greek oracles—have traditionally been women, a fact still prevailing among Gypsies. Whether their gender has contributed or not to the ruthless campaign against the exercise of clairvoyance, it is notably parallel to the patriarchal takeover in all areas of human endeavor and the drive to thrust out of our collective memory all vestiges of earlier matriarchy and the power women wielded therein. For that reason alone, it seems highly suspect to me.

To be sure, there are charlatans among psychics, formerly driven by many state laws to exercise their natural gifts in the religious context of the Spiritualist Church, but at what time have there not been charlatans among the clergy as well? Who but a charlatan baptized me into the Methodist Church? And he pales by comparison with the Jimmy Swaggarts and the Pope Alexander VI's of the world.

Perhaps there really is a genetic component to dabbling in the mystical. It admittedly takes a particular kind of mind and personality. I grew up asking questions that no one could answer to my satisfaction. In fact, I was often told that, as Anamary put it, "There are some questions we just don't ask." That may be easy for others to accept; it was impossible for me. I couldn't simply turn off my brain like an electric light. The two things that most puzzled me as a very young child were God and the government. I heard a great deal about both, but no one rendered either of them comprehensible. I eventually gave up on the government, but I kept after God for a good many years. The search took me into a lot of nooks and crannies not commonly explored by the masses.

What I found suggests the same phenomenon I have personally observed among those psychics whose "spirit guides" purportedly speak through them while they are in a state of trance. There are documented exceptions, but in my own experience, these guides—no matter what their alleged former race or nationality or level of erudition—all made precisely the same grammatical errors when they "came through" that their "channels" made when conscious; they displayed the same ignorance of the same facts, and they entertained the same biases and philosophies. That is not to say that the "messages" were always worthless and totally inaccurate. On the contrary. It *is* to say that inspiration coming from whatever repository is its source takes on the peculiar character of the individual inspired as it filters through the multiple layers of his conscious and subconscious machinations. Were this not true, the "inspired Word of God" would contain a great deal less inconsistency in Holy Writ!

To a far greater extent than most people realize, what many of them accept as religious "truth" originated with mystics not appreciably different from their modern counterparts, whether they were early Jewish Kabbalists or Christian Church Fathers. Far from being spontaneously revealed, the visions and voices most of these saw and heard came only after meditative measures still used to induce trance—from fasting to altering blood flow to the brain to intense concentration on a target object or sound—in short, practices employed as well by yogis and other Eastern mystics. Jews get an exclusively Jewish message, Christians an exclusively Christian one, and on and on.

The problem is that all such mystics, instead of recognizing the effect of input from their own minds and experiences, imagine their flights into the realm of the metaphysical to represent Absolute Truth. So much as is universally perceived by all of them probably reflects an imperfect but genuine insight into the nature of things, but the particulars that are always spelled out, often in absurd detail, are spurious at best and result in the terrible dissensions and bloodlettings that have plagued the world for ages. It intrigues me that without exception in Western society, the various religions basically agree that God is unknowable; then each of them sets about defining Him down to the very last possible attribute and function. Thereby by hangs the tail, and the tail in this instance always wags the dog, which usually ends up biting.

A perfect example is a lecture I attended by a noted Chassidic rabbi from Detroit. His subject was the coming of *Moshiach* (the Messiah) and what conditions will attend that long-awaited event. He related how all Jews will go to Jerusalem, which, to accommodate their numbers, will expand to cover the whole of Israel. Israel, in turn, will expand to cover the entire earth. A question was put to him regarding the fate of the several non-Jewish people that presently inhabit the planet. In reply, he admitted that the sages were silent on that point, since "the literature is of a very 'inward' orientation." I rest my case. So is Christian literature "inward" and Muslim.

Once in a great while, a psychic will receive information that flies directly in the face of his or her previously held beliefs. When this occurs, it's advisable to reevaluate those beliefs, as Edgar Cayce was obliged to do regarding reincarnation.

On a minor scale, such things have happened to me—not that I rate myself a psychic by any means. I have sometimes argued, as it were, with The Writing, disbelieving it, only to have it proved correct, just as I did once with the Tarot. If disturbed or puzzled by a situation I was desperate to understand in order to deal with it intelligently, I sometimes took the simple expedient of shuffling the deck in the prescribed fashion and just turning up the first three top cards as reflecting the predominant nature of present circumstances.

One time I did this and got three cards, the symbolism of which didn't seem to make sense in combination. I therefore went through the whole process again of shuffling the seventy-eight-card deck three times and cutting it once. Against astronomical odds, I peeled *the same identical three cards off the top once more!* At that point, I understood that somebody was trying to tell me something in earnest, and I spoke to my mother about what had happened. She then revealed a conversation she'd had with my husband that made the meaning of the cards fall right into place. They were providing me with invaluable advice about how to deal with a condition that I had overlooked but that was central to the problem at hand.

I have known people who claimed to talk to God every day and hear His replies. Well, I was never privileged to have such a two-way "hot line," and if I choose to employ more tangible channels of communication, that does not alter the source of the information I receive nor render it demonic.

In addition to the phobia regarding power concentrated in the hands of women, there is another likely genesis for perpetrating the notion that paranormal phenomena derive from sinister forces. These impart an undue advantage to a privileged few (picking out winning race horses is a good example) to the consequent disadvantage of others in the same way that inside information would give selected stock brokers an unfair edge. If you think about this, you begin to understand how priestly castes arose in every social system. The secrets which enabled a select few to get at hidden truths and manipulate events had to be closely guarded to ensure that they would be used only in what was believed by the elite to be most beneficial to all.

If paranormal expertise were equally distributed to all humankind, it would threaten a fantastic sort of anarchy inimical to the social control traditionally held by religious and civil authorities. Many who believe information about UFOs is deliberately being withheld from the population at large by the government do so on the basis of this very premise. Imagine a world, for example, in which the ability of a Uri Geller to interfere with what we comprehend as natural law was understood and commonly held. "Stone walls" would quite literally not "a prison make, nor iron bars a cage." During group experiments with Dr. John Thomas Richards, I have personally witnessed the most extraordinary levitations of heavy material objects in my own home that were not even being touched by a human agent. If I'd had recourse to whatever antigravitational mechanism is involved when I was a high-school teacher several years ago, I would have been sorely tempted to levitate some of my more difficult students right out the window!

The word "medicine" means "controlled poison," and many of the same things that cure will, in greater quantities, kill. The key to human well-being lies in that gray, debated area of what constitutes proper control, and every religion has a slightly different answer, none of them really adequate to the problem of inculcating in the nature of man the ability to restrict himself *voluntarily* to the benign application of those energies that lie dormant both within and without. The "evil" with which the paranormal is potentially fraught is more apt to come from inside us than from some nether world. As Hill and Williams point out in *The Supernatural*, the difference between incantations addressed to angels and those invoking demons is largely one of intent. *Daemon est Deus inversus.*

One man's god is another man's devil, usually for no other reason than the fact that they bear different names. Allegations of "false gods" are analogous to saying that a dog isn't a dog if it's known as a *hund* (German) or *perro* (Spanish), and "idols" have ordinarily served as "visual aids" that transpose esoteric mysteries into simple concepts that can be grasped by the unsophisticated masses to keep them in line rather than physical objects to be worshipped in and of themselves.

If, historically, the masses have treated them literally rather than symbolically, that does not invalidate the wisdom that lay behind the concept from which they were derived. Slavish, unreasoning adherence to religious ritual even in these times is nothing but a variation on the theme of idol worship, for it attaches an importance to physical acts and objects that bears no relation to the nature of divinity. Every Old Testament prophet railed against such abuse, just as Jesus did.

In view of widespread misunderstanding and consequent hatred, why *should* we be trusted with indiscriminate power to bring about change that would affect others as well as ourselves when we cannot even agree on what is "good" and what is "bad"? In its tendency to particularize and exclude, to assign a designation of *fact* to mere *supposition*, religion has failed abysmally to foster permanent improvements in human behavior. Too much is tacked on to the natural benefits deriving from genuine good will towards others—too many codicils, too many conditions. The result has been a kind of "country-club morality," applicable only to souls of the same general description. Anything that seems to contradict or undermine such exclusivity is considered harmful and therefore anathema. Historically, its adherents are shunned or put to death as apostates.

A collection of sermons by Charles Grandison Finney, the Nineteenth-Century father of American evangelism, includes one in which he projects a view of heaven from which the saved look down upon the damned in hell, where he has these unfortunates writhing in graphic descriptions of eternal agony. The fact that a man calling himself a Christian could imagine a place of reputed bliss in which the departed can observe the inexpressible suffering of others—many no doubt known and once loved by them—with no measure of sorrow or pity to dim their supreme happiness is perhaps the ultimate expression of arrogant self-righteousness and hardness of heart. It is a short step from that ability to one of having no pity for "lesser" *living* mortals and is of a piece with the millennia-long practice among religious groups of going forth to slaughter one and all who do not subscribe to their particular creeds. It is instructive to know that Finney's good Christians are looking down at Roman Catholics, Mormons, and—worst of all—Universalists, the religion of Alcott's March family in *Little Women*. A word to the wise....

As lately as 1949, when I was hospitalized at Barnes, it was commonly believed in the part of Texas where my very "Christian" (adult) roommate grew up that Blacks don't even have souls. The implication, of course, is that lacking a soul capable of being saved *or* damned, they can be treated as nothing but animals with complete impunity on the part of their oppressors.

Any way you look at it, institutionalized religion has been responsible for more violence and suffering than any other single human force in history. That the paranormal is reviled as being *evil* in comparison is both ludicrous and insupportable.

The hysterical hue and cry against "humanism" among fundamentalist sects of Christians and Jews (Muslims too, I suppose) is proof positive of barriers against some basic, universal understanding that holds, as our Founding Fathers did, "certain Truths to be self-evident." Contrary to popular opinion, these were not *religious "truths"*; they were basic natural laws derived from cause-and-effect evidence. Right-wing Fundamentalists regard it as an outrage that Huckleberry Finn can come to the right ethical decisions by searching his own good heart rather than following a Sunday-school formula that says he should never lie, and they demand that he—along with such fellows as many of Shakespeare's characters endowed with the same ability—be banished from textbooks and libraries. Nor are they alone in their moral myopia. Ultra-religious Jews hold that the only valid reason for any particular behavior, be it ever so obviously necessary to human welfare, is that God commanded it. They are strictly forbidden to do anything on the mere basis of its natural consequences.

This rigid obduracy actually runs counter to a favorite analogy often drawn between God's relationship to man and a father's relationship to his children. When a child is too young to grasp the intellectual niceties of certain desirable conduct or lacks the practical experience to identify danger, the rationale of "because I said so" is proper and sufficient, but as he grows older, absolute parental authority is ideally supplanted by such reasoning and guidance as will permit him to understand what rational justification lies behind the command or the proscription. He is then able to make intelligent choices that have relevance and meaning to life, not only in terms of his own welfare, but also that of others.

Strangely enough, the same religious Jews who side with fundamentalist Christians in respect to humanism purport to believe that one of the changes to be ushered in with the Messianic Era is that mankind will not require instruction in morality, but that "the Law" will be written in each heart. But perhaps it is there already—not a "Law" consisting of 613 *mitzvoth,* or commandments (of which *The Ten* are just that—ten), but one comprehended by Hinduism and Buddhism as that nebulous conscience in each individual which is a karmic memory of past lessons painfully learned in other lives. That it is so often ignored does not militate against its presence. I knew it was wrong to take Bette's kitten, or I would not have hidden it in Mother's bedroom. What seems necessary is not an addition to our moral baggage, but the elimination of certain traits like greed that frequently recruit "moral principles" to implement their ends.

Those who decry various movements today lumped together indiscriminately under the heading of "New Age" or "Aquarian Age" apparently fail to see in them an almost wistful impulse toward the very universality of love and compassion implicit in the messianic vision. The paranormal evinces no creeds, erects no dogmatic barriers to participation in its several manifestations. It thus offers more hope, for it is quite possible that intrinsic to it is an immediate built-in punishment for abusing it, just as there is long-term corrective punishment (as well as reward) over the course of many lives in the concept of reincarnation.

It was finally through the paranormal, outside the usual confines of religious experience, that I learned the nature of true spirituality and found peace. My "time for white roses" was also my initiation into the meaning of life, which—ironically—starts with a proper understanding of death.

CHAPTER ELEVEN

My folks were visiting me in Arizona the May during which Anamary's seventy-ninth birthday fell. We celebrated with all the usual trappings, but there was just a hint of sadness about the occasion, for Anamary was convinced that the event heralded the imminent end of her life. I tried to cheer her up by saying she couldn't die on an uneven number; nevertheless, when I saw everyone on the train back to Missouri, my heart was gripped by a fear that our good-byes would be the last. Two years later when I myself returned there following a divorce, she was still going strong, and after I decided to move into a house I had bought and rented out, she worked like a woman a third of her age helping me fix it up.

    I was inside painting one day while she hung screens outside on the long, old-fashioned windows. I went out onto the porch for something just in time to see her step backwards off the edge of it holding a screen with both hands. She crashed to the ground, her left hip taking the full brunt of the fall. It was broken, as we both instantly feared, and the fracture had to be reduced with surgery and the insertion of metal pins. She was then eighty-three, and because of her age as well as the degree of arthritic fixation observed in her joints, her doctor offered her little hope of walking again. Undaunted, she not only walked without artificial aids, but she even went back to her previous custom of doing laundry in the basement and carrying heavy baskets of wash up the steps to hang outside to dry. When I had another child, she carried him around long after he could walk and became to both my young sons all she had been to me.

It is to my second husband's credit that he shared my affection for "the girls" and offered no resistance when Mother and I agreed upon the merger that would make it possible for us all to live under one large roof after Dad's death. The proposal promised to be no more beneficial to Mother and Anamary than it would be to me. Both were still in full command of their faculties and, though obviously fragile, still mobile and able to carry on pretty much as usual, if on a somewhat limited scale. Mother's hands were terribly crippled with arthritis and correspondingly painful, but she gritted her teeth and kept using them, balancing pots and pans on her wrists and proudly declining such help as was offered in the course of her daily activities.

By the time our arrangement was realized in the form of a new house on eight acres of land in the country, my third son was two. Had it not been for the elders in residence there, I couldn't have continued my education as I did, nor could my second husband have spent three years in graduate school several hundred miles away.

The advantages were reciprocal, of course. Shortly after we moved in together and ten years after her first hip fracture, Anamary fell again and broke the other hip. This time she was ninety-three, and the prognosis was even bleaker than before. Again she defied expectations based on the best medical evidence and walked following convalescence, but with a walker for the most part. That was only the first of a series of catastrophes, however. When she was ninety-six, a duodenal ulcer of which we were unaware perforated, resulting in peritonitis. I had been taking her to an internist regularly. Every time we were there, she mentioned that her stomach hurt, but the only thing he did was prescribe something on the order of antacids available across the counter.

Nothing was done the night I drove her to the emergency room of the nearest hospital, twenty-five miles away, except to give her pain medication. By the time I went back the next morning, she had been X-rayed, and the diagnosis was certain. A surgeon came in and sat on the edge of her bed. He was kind and as gentle as it was possible to be under the circumstances, but the truth was harsh. Anamary expressed doubts that she could survive surgery at her age, and he candidly agreed that the odds were not in her favor. He pointed out the obvious, though: it was a foregone conclusion that she couldn't live with a hole in her stomach!

After he left to make the necessary preparations for operating immediately, we were alone to think the unthinkable and say, as best we could, the unsayable. I promised at Anamary's request not to tell Mother what was happening until it was all over. The original plan had been for me to return home and bring her back to visit in the afternoon. As soon as Anamary was taken to the OR, I called and explained that she was under medication and out of pain and that it would be better just to let her sleep. I said I would wait until she woke up so I could tell more about how she felt before I came home. Then began a solitary and difficult vigil.

I waited in a small room off the Intensive Care Unit near the surgical wing. There wasn't anything but the agony of a blinding sinus headache to distract me from the agony in my heart and the very loneliness of a Gethsemane. I could think of nothing but the fact that I was not ready to lose the dearest friend I'd ever had. About two hours into eternity, I went out to pace the hall just as double doors swung open and a patient was wheeled through them on a bed. It was Anamary. She looked up and smiled at me as she passed by. I smiled back and winked as if we had just prevailed in a conspiracy to play an enormous joke on the devil himself.

She lived on, that wonderful, indomitable woman. She recovered and came home, played "cars" with my youngest, fretted if the middle one stayed too long at the creek on his frequent rambles, and worried that the oldest would die of heat stroke mowing the lawn. It is a sad commentary on the ethical standards all too evident in the medical profession that the internist, who was as least indirectly responsible for the perforation, charged more for coming into the hospital room once a day, grunting something unintelligible which he scribbled in her chart (probably illegibly) and then disappearing than did the surgeon who saved her life and then also called on her daily. We continued to be billed by the former for fees over and above Medicare coverage. I consulted an attorney about suing for malpractice, but alas. Pain and suffering unnecessarily inflicted on the old are not compensable, since they have so short a life expectancy. Infuriated, I finally wrote the internist a letter expressing myself in carefully chosen words, told him what to do with the next bill, and just hoped the envelope would not spontaneously combust before delivery. Apparently it didn't, for we never received any more statements.

I became somewhat adept at recognizing the thud of falling bodies. It sounds like nothing else. Anamary sustained another tumble that resulted in a broken wrist, but she weathered it too with the same courage that informed everything else she did. We were her life, and when, in 1980, just two years short of her century mark, I planned to relocate in Oregon on the eve of yet another divorce, it was she who said emphatically, "As long as I'm alive, I want to be where June and the boys are." Mother would have preferred to remain in Missouri with a niece, but her attachment to and sense of responsibility for her sister disallowed any choice but to join her in that determination.

So it was that in April of 1981, when Anamary was just a month away from being ninety-nine and Mother was ninety, they took their first airplane ride to another Salem, far away from that small Missouri community by the same name near which they had both been born. I got seats for us as close as possible to a lavatory and managed somehow to squeeze in with Anamary to help out when she needed its facilities. Sardines, by comparison, have elbowroom to spare. As we were deplaning in Portland, a stranger who had also been on the flight approached me and identified herself as a geriatric nurse.

"I just want to comment," she said, "on the way you have cared for these women during the trip. I see so many elderly people who are abused that it makes my heart glad when someone is patient and loving with them." It had never occurred to me that I might be doing anything out of the ordinary.

Because my apartment was on the second floor and the stairs were too difficult for Anamary to negotiate, I got her and Mother another apartment in the building adjacent to mine. We fixed up a room for my middle son there so someone would always be on hand at night should an emergency arise, and through the social services of the State of Oregon, an aide was obtained who came through the day, bathed Anamary, and did light housekeeping chores. I was able to land a three-year track appointment to the faculty of Oregon State University in the English Department and commuted to Corvallis three days a week, and life continued pretty much as it had been in Missouri. We were just slightly more spread out.

Anamary still worried about everyone's welfare, so it was customary for my children and me to check in with her on arriving home from wherever we had been. She was particularly anxious respecting our whereabouts after dark, and if Danny, who was then nine, happened to fail to report in, she would get on the phone after Mother dialed our number and ask if he was home. Since her hearing was severely impaired, it was useless to answer, but for some reason I always tried, thereby alerting everybody in the neighborhood but her as to his safety. Invariably he was sent over in person to set her mind at ease, although crossing a driveway and climbing a flight of steps back to our place somewhat nullified the effect of his reassurance!

Despite this constant fretting, she forgot his name one day and asked Mother, "What's your little boy's name?"

"You mean Danny?" Mother asked.

"Yes. That's it," she replied, adding, "My little boy's name is Charles."

Charles was already pushing six feet tall, but as far as she was concerned, he was still the Charles she had carried around years before to the tune of our protestations.

This living arrangement still obtained when Anamary reached her one-hundredth birthday. A nephew and one of his sons, along with the latter's wife and children, flew in from Georgia, and we celebrated as befitted the occasion. Notified in advance, the then President Ronald Reagan and First Lady Nancy sent felicitations, which Anamary didn't much value, and the local press covered the event with customary hit-or-miss accuracy. The reporter did get one thing right: when asked to recall the happiest day of her long life, Anamary quickly responded, "The day they told me I had a baby sister." After four brothers, that must indeed have been welcome news.

It was, and still is, mind-boggling to contemplate the changes that single lifetime embraced. Anamary was a grown young woman before the first automobile appeared on the scene, and roughly twenty years before her death, she had watched a man walk on the surface of the moon by virtue of another technological miracle, television. Never again will it be necessary for any given individual to accommodate himself to such extreme transformations, for developments between 1882 and 1982 expanded the scope of *possibility* to the farthest reaches of human imagination. We are now a people inured to surprise, for the fantastic is now the commonplace.

In a very real way, Anamary was a "woman for all seasons," a woman of sense and sensibility, of intelligence and intuition. She had always been the family database, serving as the last word on who did what when. Even at a hundred her memory of the distant past was incredible. What she could have done with her mind, given a different chance in life, strains the fancy to conceive.

Not only had she always been the repository of historical date, but she always knew where everything was—often, I suppose, because she had put it there herself. An orderly house, someone once told me, reflects an orderly mind in the housekeeper, and I believe that to be irrefutable fact. As one who has wasted at least half her life looking for keys, spectacles, umbrellas, phone bills (and sometimes the phone), shoes and nail clippers, I can attest to the correlation and its corresponding antithesis. I'll never forget, after all she'd been through in the stomach surgery, how Anamary was able days later to recall where the nurse (who was looking for them) had put her dentures when she moved her belongings to ICU before the operation.

My physician, for whom I otherwise had the utmost respect, opined after Mother and Anamary moved in with me that I had a "neurotic sense of responsibility" and that it would be far better if my girls were vegetables and could be relegated to a nursing facility. That is cold-blooded and unmitigated hogwash. To have lived without the laughter, the overt evidence of human courage, the example of patient forbearance with the foibles of others that these two provided would have left all the rest of us in the family impoverished to exactly the extent that we were privileged to become enriched by their presence in our daily lives. Their even-handed sense of fairness and their capacity to judge between the insignificant and the truly important kept petty crises in perspective and made us a little more sane and a lot more considerate of one another.

If I chafed sometimes that I was not accorded proper acknowledgement of my adulthood, the irritation was counterbalanced by the comfort of having someone care where and how I was. My husband was still away at graduate school the year I turned forty, and my best friend (a divorcee close to my age) took me out to dinner and a floor show. When I dropped her off at her house, I went in to phone Mother so she would know I was then on my way home, It was eleven o'clock. With some spirit, she said, "It's about time!"

I couldn't resist. "Do you know how old I am today, Mother?" I asked her. But I'm not sure that ever really registered with her. I was always her child and, *ipso facto*, required looking after. Once a mother, always a mother. That came home to me the winter day I walked up to my oldest son on the campus of Washington University and, in the presence of a young lady engaged in conversation with him, proceeded to button the top two buttons of his shirt.

In spite of all this, Mother never interfered when I made a shamble of things. She didn't even rub it in when she helped me pick up the pieces.

In the fall after Anamary reached a hundred, I decided it would be more convenient if we were all under the same roof again, so we rented a house together, and Mother was relieved of preparing meals. She retained her sense of usefulness by doing dishes and waiting on Anamary. The move was timely. Anamary was hospitalized in November with pneumonia and seemed to go downhill from that point on. Accustomed to garrulous, crotchety old people, the hospital personnel were astonished at her sweet disposition and her willing cooperation. I remarked to her once that if someone had come in and said, "Here, Anamary, take this strychnine," she would have smiled and replied, "Okay."

This characteristic is germane to something I've observed across the board. People do not change as they grow older: they just become "more so." Whatever the predominant traits, they are accentuated with the passing of time. Old resentments, long buried under habits of civility, will often surface then and seem to reflect major alterations in attitude when, in fact, the only change is a relaxation of former restraints. The cantankerous senior citizen had a head start earlier on. My children are therefore advised to watch out!

I understand that not every personality lends itself to the arrangement the girls and I enjoyed. Mothers-in-law have crossed my path whose constant company I could not have endured for more than twenty-four hours, if that long. Even my situation sometimes grew burdensome, but that was largely because of the perennial poverty that dogged my heels with merciless persistence. The boys and I could never all go out together at the same time in the evening, for one of us always had to "ladysit." The likelihood that one of our frail charges would fall or even die was too great to risk leaving them alone.

There was also the matter of Mother's fiercely independent nature that sometimes created all sorts of problems. Even when an aide or the rest of us were present, she steadfastly refused to ask for help in moving Anamary's wheelchair from one place to another towards the last when it was difficult for her to walk.

Because Mother's hands were so crippled by arthritis, she couldn't manipulate it very well, and one day it hung up on the edge of a rug, tipped forward, and dumped its occupant out in the floor. No harm was done, except to my nervous system, which was fairly fragile along then. It was not strengthened by my teenager, Charles, whose Rock band practiced in the garage and who seemed to think he had been deprived of an inalienable right to be born to wealthy parents.

The last Christmas we were all together, the only meat I had to serve was hamburger, which had to be stretched as far as possible. To Charles' disgust, I turned it into meatloaf. His reaction was such that my portion became cold while I wept in the bathroom. It shouldn't have mattered so much, but that's much easier to say now than it was to realize then. He more than made up for his insensitivity a short time later and did a great deal of growing up in the process.

I quipped to a social worker one day that I was immortal, since Mother wouldn't die till Anamary did, Anamary wouldn't die till I did, and I couldn't die till they both did. The three of us were caught in a web of love and mutual dependence that precluded both the freedom to live and the freedom not to. The last thing Mother and Anamary wanted on earth was to be a burden to anyone. To precisely the extent that they realized they had become burdens to me, they felt unhappy, and to the extent that I realized they were, I felt guilty and ashamed.

The terrible ambivalence of that time was soul racking. There were no good solutions to any of the problems that confronted us. It was one thing to have an Anamary still functional and self-reliant, but quite another to have to watch her deteriorate physically and suffer mentally because of the resulting helplessness.

Poverty was only part of the problem. There was still my own precarious health, pushed to the breaking point by the demands on my limited strength. Lecturing and breathing in chalk dust on a regular basis often left me unable to speak at the end of the days on which I taught. Then there were roughly a hundred student compositions to grade per week. I myself had just been released from the hospital following pneumonia the week before Anamary was admitted with the same thing that bleak November. Mine was a foregone conclusion. I drove Charles' VW Bug to work, since it got better gas mileage than my pickup truck. Its windshield wipers didn't work, nor its heater. It was inevitable that the fall and winter, even for Oregon, would be exceptionally wet that year. I think it rained every day I was scheduled to teach.

Someone told me to smear a halved raw potato on the glass so the water would sheet instead of bead up. It worked, but I still came to think of the world as a vast blur that season—a vast *cold* blur. In spite of everything, for a person who had been told by the medical pros twenty years before never to go to school again nor seek gainful employment, I wasn't doing too badly. A doctor back then—Dr. Ogura, in fact—had all but written me a prescription for a rich husband and wanted to fix me up with another patient of his in 1954—a Cadillac dealer from California. Oh, well.

I remember playing the piano a lot when I should have been doing other things during that awful period and diligently memorizing something by Debussy as if nothing else mattered. And there was laughter, though I have trouble recalling why. I do recollect Danny's hanging around the facing of the kitchen door minutes after I came home from the hospital to tell me about a cute yellow kitten he had seen at school. It looked hungry, he said.

"Why didn't you bring it home with you?" I asked him.

At that, he sheepishly thrust it forward from where he had been concealing it behind him. Come to think of it, I also remember the chuckles Mother and I had privately at the expense of a male aide we were sent for a while. When he wasn't singing hymns to the girls, he was elaborating on his work history in excruciating detail. He had been employed, among other strange places, in a crematorium. Jolly sort of companion for the aged.

One morning in January, Anamary awoke unable to talk intelligibly. She apparently thought she was communicating normally, yet it was impossible to understand her. Her affect was unchanged, though. Her eyes and her smile were still as responsive as ever. But it was heartrending. I had a chronic compulsion to slam my fist through a wall and scream invectives at the deaf universe. Instead I smiled back, combed and plaited her long hair as I always had when she was ill, gave her juice when she probably wanted water and vice versa, and promised my boys I would not live a whole century. I had never before made an issue of being adopted, but I got so infernally sick of people's congratulating me on my prospective, genetically engineered longevity that I began announcing my disclaimer to any expectation of that particular "blessing" as a matter, almost, of self-defense. Thanks, but no thanks. Why so many people whose professed yearning is to go to heaven don't want to die to get there is a puzzlement.

I knew Anamary wanted to die at home, and I had given my word that she would be permitted to do so. When she became dehydrated later that month and began having chest rales, I was faced with making the first of many agonizing decisions that were necessary during the course of the then fledgling 1983. Should I—*could* I—let Nature take its course, or should I send her to the hospital? How long would it be possible to stave off the inevitable? What was the kindest thing to do? Mother was not in favor of the hospital, but she deferred to my judgment. I could accept Anamary's death now, but not death drawn out in a slow, struggling, painful disintegration.

Whether for my sake or hers, I had her admitted to the hospital and stayed with her every possible minute, for she was far beyond the ability to use a call light and could not have articulated her needs in any event. Nurses could speak to her and shake her arm all they liked; she would lie there with her eyes closed, to all appearances unconscious, but I had only to say, "Anamary," and those eyes flew open, searching for mine. She would not eat for anyone else.

Her chest cleared up, and the hospital would not keep her beyond ten days. Because she was still on an IV, the doctor had her transferred to a nursing home nearby. I wasn't happy about that, but I acquiesced for the time being. The third day she was there, I took Danny with me to see her. It was his first encounter with the almost suffocating odor of disinfectant, the whimpers of the old and terminally ill, the institutional drabness of the décor, the vacuous stares of faded rheumy eyes, the frail misshapen bodies bound to wheelchairs, and the unmistakable scent of decaying flesh that even the disinfectant could not mask. He summed it up in a word: "This is terrible!" he exclaimed.

"Look around you and remember," I told him, "and promise you'll never put me in such a place as this."

He promised with all the sincerity an eleven-year-old can express.

Anamary was sleeping, a tray of juice and Jello untouched on the table beside her. The juice was warm and the Jello melting. I checked the condition of her bed linens. She was lying in a mess of feces so old it had dried. I could have killed at that instant.

"That's it!" I said. "You're going home, baby!"

Getting her out was about as easy as springing an inmate from Leavenworth. Her doctor was not to be found, and release required his permission.

"Like hell!" I told the dragon at the gate. "I'll sign her out myself and take full responsibility for the consequences."

This must not have been done too frequently, for my firm resolution created all kinds of bureaucratic panic, in spite of which I fully intended to leave with my aunt if I had to remove the IV myself and drag her outside on a sheet with Danny's help. She was only eighty pounds of skin stretched over bone, but I knew from lifting her many times a day for weeks that her tiny frame was more than I could carry in my arms. Drastic measures proved unnecessary. It's amazing what can be done when people discover they have to do it! I got her released without coming to blows with anyone and engaged an ambulance to take her home. She understood what was happening and brightened up appreciably back in her own room and her own bed, gratitude and happiness glowing in her smiles. The State authorized funding for a live-in aide to relieve the strain we were under, particularly at night, and there was little left to do but try to make Anamary as comfortable as possible and wait out the clock. That was more easily said than done, however.

I was sitting beside her a couple of days after her homecoming when she looked past me and spoke as if addressing someone else in the room. It was the first time in weeks that she had said anything distinct and coherent.

"Open the door and let me go through," she urged. There was a pause before she looked directly at me to explain, "I can't go."

Those were the last words she would utter. A short time later she lapsed into a sleep from which we unanimously agreed not to attempt waking her, although we continued turning her every two hours and keeping her clean. The rales returned, audible all over the house, and it was obvious from the solid matter in her catheter bag that her kidney tissue was breaking down. I worried that she might be conscious of hunger or thirst and sometimes held a cotton ball soaked in water to her lips. She would suck on it, and then I'd feel even worse, certain that, in fact, she was aware of needs she couldn't convey.

Anger and grief contended for control over my emotions. Why couldn't that brave heart just shut down the way everything else was doing? I longed to stop it myself, longed to open that door of her brief vision. Who was denying her passage through it, and why? Why, why, why, why? Rage was futile and love powerless it seemed.

As if to prove that her fury was far from exhausted, Fate lashed out with a new vengeance. On a Sunday, the third day into Anamary's coma, Mother fell ill with pneumonia and had to be admitted to the hospital. In addition, our aide, that same day, returned home to Eugene to pick up some more clothing. While she was there, her car broke down, and she called to say she would not be able to get back in the foreseeable future. I think it was Goethe who wrote, "As flies to wanton boys are we to the gods. They kill us for their sport." He was wrong. They continually push us off cliffs, catching us scant inches from the boulders below, and take us back up to push us off again to potential death. Wondering on the way down if the net will be there constitutes the agonizing tension between hope and despair that summarizes the human condition. Killing is merciful by comparison.

I sat up with Anamary almost all that night, though I knew I had no choice but go to work the next day. I had already lost far too much time. I couldn't have slept anyway. The silence, broken only by her loud breathing, was so oppressive that I began to talk to her, just as if she could hear and understand me. I told her as nearly as I could how very much she had meant to me and how I would gladly have died *for* her had it been possible. Anything to alleviate the terrible struggle in which she was painfully locked. I asked her to come back to me once it was over—begged her to let me know in some way if the spirit really does survive its corporeal dwelling. I wanted indisputable proof.

There was no other alternative on Monday but to keep Charles, then barely seventeen, out of school to stay home and take over for me, knowing full well what he might be required to do. I left written instructions and went over them with him. It would not be easy, but he must straighten her legs and be sure her eyes were closed. There was a list of phone numbers in the order of importance.

I returned to my office from a one o'clock class to find a message from him to call home. When I did, he said simply and quietly, "She's gone." I had known that, and I planned to be relieved, but my heart hadn't gotten the word. It broke, not only for Anamary, but for that courageous boy who had done what few adults are ever called upon to do and had done it manfully.

CHAPTER TWELVE

It was February 7, three days after my unremarked and cheerless forty-eighth birthday. One of the most difficult tasks still lay ahead: Mother had to be told. The boys and I went to the hospital, but it was some time before I could get a sufficient grip on myself to go in and say what had to be said. Only once had I seen my mother cry, but I was made of a cheap alloy compared to her iron.

When we had finally trooped into her room, our greetings were happy enough, but our presence there together was revealing.

"How's Anamary?" Mother asked immediately. There was an edge to the question that sounded like a challenge. She expected the truth. I took hold of her hand.

"She's fine now."

She sighed a long, deep, quivering sigh.

"Poor old girl," she said. "I'm glad she's out of it."

Her strength supported us, as it always had when the chips were down.

Everything had been arranged in advance, even to the eulogy I had written which would be read at Anamary's funeral. I wouldn't have let a clergyman touch that tribute with a proverbial ten-foot pole, for I had remained sitting through the one delivered over Jay Walter only as a courtesy to the people there who loved him. The preacher had all but said he was damned to hell for never having "accepted Christ as his personal savior" and held him up to the rest of us as a tragic example. Walter had lived vibrantly into his nineties and wanted, for some reason, to reach a hundred and fifteen, but cancer got to him before he got to his goal. Some Bible-toting do-gooder was always trying to save his soul towards the end. He sent one of them packing with a profundity I still cherish as saying everything that needs to be said.

"If there's a just God," he told the fellow, "I don't have anything to worry about. If there isn't, it wouldn't do any good to worry."

It was also he who told me once when we were discussing politics that he had lived long enough to be wrong about everything. He was one in ten million. He also told me that the next best thing to a beautiful woman is beautiful horse. Who could argue with priorities like that? He also loved flowers—especially brightly colored ones—and had a bed of gladioli every year that was his pride and joy.

Until Anamary came to live with us, Mother had kept my hair cut in a Dutch-boy bob. I don't recall doing so, but I have no reason to doubt reports that I threw a fit every time she trimmed it. This was apparently more than Anamary could stand, for she offered to assume responsibility for my hair if Mother would let it grow. She had herself a deal. From then on, she rolled it up in rags every night in such a way that I had sausage curls the next day. Why I preferred that bedtime ritual and sleeping on a bunch of hard lumps to the freedom of short hair will never be known.

I incurred a considerable debt to her for these ministrations, but it was one of the few such obligations I was able to repay. Every time she was hospitalized or convalescing, I had faithfully taken care of her hair every day and usually twice a day. I knew that no one else could arrange it to her satisfaction and that one last installment was due on the balance of my outstanding account. I instructed the mortician merely to wash her hair and leave the styling to me when everything else was ready for her to be sent back to Missouri.

Danny wanted, in effect, to say goodbye, for he had been at school when she died and was taken away. He went with me to do what had to be done, and I was grateful for his company in addition to his help: he held hairpins and provided invaluable diversion. It was a frustrating and difficult job quite apart from the obvious aspects of the situation, and I had, besides, five thumbs on each sweaty hand. Hair clung to them and came out of its assigned place, combs refused to stay put, and pins kept falling to the floor. In retrospect, it was altogether hilarious, and if Anamary was looking on from her new dimension, she must have laughed heartily.

"It's dogged as does it." Anamary took her second airplane ride looking exactly as she would have wished to look. I flew back to Missouri to the funeral and was joined there by my oldest son, Bruce, who came down from Wisconsin, where he was in graduate school. I had asked each of the boys to write a special message on the card that accompanied their respective floral gifts. His thanked her for the patience he would never forget.

The husband of a dear friend from high-school days had kindly consented to conduct the service in his capacity as a lay-minister and read the prepared eulogy. One of his daughters was to sing the musical selections, among them "Goin' Home," a Negro spiritual incorporated by Anton Dvorak into his *New World Symphony*. There is no more beautiful a concept of death expressed anywhere than in its lyrics, which seemed singularly appropriate to Anamary, for whom the "door jus' close by" had finally opened. When its time came in the program, I rose from my seat and approached the podium.

"I realize this is highly irregular," I said, "and I many not make it all the way through. If I don't, I'm sure you will understand, but this is something I have to do."

It was the last thing I could give Anamary of myself, and I sang for her with my heart, knowing somehow that the words of the song were true—that she was "jus' a-livin' on," her "work all done and care laid by."

Later on a hill in the outskirts of Dexter from which one could see across to a field where once had stood the house where Anamary had lived when her family first moved to Stoddard County, I watched her body laid to rest beside her mother's in the Caroline Dowdy Cemetery, named after a close family friend with whose children she and Mother had played as youngsters. I knew that someday I would lie beside her, for that is where I would belong. But I also knew, as I turned for one last, long look before departing, that I did not really leave her there. Suffused with that certainty, I went back to Oregon with renewed courage.

Mother was released from the hospital shortly afterwards, and I immediately sent her by plane to visit her only remaining brother in Arizona. They had not seen each other for about twenty years, and I knew this would be the last opportunity for them to meet again. She was gone, therefore, when I awoke in the act of bolting from the bed on the night of February 13. The boys were sound asleep in their room.

Whatever had wakened me was still hitting the roof, describing a diagonal path across the ceiling. Alternately striking and bouncing, it sounded as if it would crash right through: *Bam! Bam! Bam! Bam! Bam!* the object went five times before it reached the edge of the roof and bounced off. I dashed to the window underneath its apparent point of exit. We lived on a corner lot then with an unobstructed view of the intersecting streets, well lit by a streetlamp. It was coming one of those slow winter rains common to Oregon, and there was nothing stirring outside—not a person, not a car, not an animal—nothing. There wasn't even an airplane going over. I glanced at the clock as I ran from the room to check the rest of the house. It was a few minutes after midnight and technically February 14, Valentine's Day.

My inspection of the back yard yielded no more information than the empty street had. Maggie, our Irish setter, hadn't uttered a sound and seemed nonplused by my agitated nocturnal activity. Still somewhat shaken, I finally returned to bed and had barely gone back to sleep when it was time to get up and go to work. The first thing I did was look out to see what, if any, evidence there was to explain the night's unusual disturbance.

Surrounding the house was a five-foot or so swath of bare dirt containing shrubbery. In more prosperous times, it had been covered with bark dust, but this had long since become one with the soil.

Directly in front of my window, right at the edge of this strip before the grass began, there was a sizable rock that I didn't recall ever noticing previously. I marked its location in the dim light of dawn and promised myself to have a look at it when I came home that evening.

It was dark by the time I returned, so Danny and I took a flashlight out to locate and examine my find. The rock had obviously been the projectile, for it had struck the wet ground so hard it had thrown up a rim of mud all round itself as it became imbedded to a depth of about an inch. I took it in and laid it up, intending to scrutinize it carefully later on, for I had brought home an armload of papers to grade that could not be put off. Sometime later that night, as I was propped up in bed surrounded by piles of compositions, Charles came into my room with a strange expression on his face.

"Look at this, Mom" he said, handing me the rock.

He had washed off the mud and made an interesting discovery. On one face of it was a distinct letter "A" that appeared almost white against the charcoal gray matrix of the rock itself. The rounded part that formed the top was glazed, as if that portion had melted under the influence of intense heat. I had read about such things attributed to poltergeists, but a rock with an "A" on it strongly suggested more than any old noisy ghost!

"Here's my answer!" I told Charles triumphantly, cradling the rock in my hand as if it had been the Hope diamond. I believed then, and I believe now, that Anamary somehow contrived to send it in response to the pleas I made that last night she lived. Not only did she zero in on our house, but that part of it in which she knew I was sleeping. I was impressed and jubilant. Was she reminding me of my encounter with the "Philistines" as a child, saying, in effect, "I can't walk you to school anymore, but keep this stone in your pocket as proof that I'm still around to protect you"?

Anticipating that some skeptic would say this treasure was no more than a meteorite, lacking any apparent terrestrial mechanism for its forceful descent onto my roof, I took it to the Geology Department of Oregon State University the next day and submitted it to one of the professors there for analysis of its composition and probable origin. No problem. He identified it immediately as being volcanic material of a kind indigenous to the Northwest and explained how the tiny flecks of feldspar were formed. It is a very old rock, he said, whose smooth, rounded contours had resulted from the action of water on its surface over a long, long period. Perhaps it had come from the Coast. He offered no explanation for the "A"—which he, too, clearly recognized.

Trying another tack, I later took it to a psychic who cupped her hands around its fairly hefty bulk (it weighs nine ounces and measures three and a half inches at its longest dimension) and told me, as had the professor, that it is very old. She sensed that it had been used in some sort of "circle"—not like ours," she added, meaning by "ours" those groups that gathered weekly at the local Spiritualist Church to hear messages from a medium. After a bit, she also said that it contains "a lot of healing power." Somehow this did not surprise me in the least. Surely the energy—whatever its kind or source—necessary to dropping it from a goodly height onto my roof (not to mention transporting it a considerable distance in all probability) would have permeated the object. How to release it was another question altogether.

Curious about the force with which the missile had struck the roof hard enough to bounce six times instead of merely rolling, Danny and I climbed on top of the house to see if any evidence of impact remained. We found an indentation in the asphalt shingles that precisely fitted one of the rock's distinctively shaped ends. It was located near the ridge at an angle to my bedroom window that would exactly account for the path I heard the racket describe over my ceiling. The roofing was fairly new and revealed no other such irregularities.

Nothing else out of the ordinary happened—until a month later. I was again awakened abruptly out of a deep sleep only minutes after midnight on the morning of March 14. What I heard that time sounded as if someone was in my bathroom having diarrhea! Water—or something liquid, at any rate—would gush into the commode with a resulting splash, then after a moment or two of silence, gush again. This was repeated over and over. I first thought of Danny, but then I noticed that he had gotten into bed with me sometime in the night and was curled up there sound asleep. Anamary's death had an understandably unsettling effect on him, and he required patient indulgence of his insecurities. Charles had gone out on a date earlier, so I then assumed that he had come home and wondered why he was using my bathroom instead of the one off the hall. The noise persisted, and I called out—I thought to him.

"Charles, are you sick?" I asked.

There was no answer. Alarmed, I got up and started to look in on him, but when I passed my window, I saw that the truck was still gone. He wasn't even home yet! Mystified, I went on into the bathroom. Not a trickle of water was running anywhere, and the semblance of splashing stopped as I entered. I waited several minutes. When it did not recur, I returned to bed and mulled over the implications of the phenomenon. This was no dream, by the way! It suddenly occurred to me that the last month Anamary was still up on her feet using her walker, she had been plagued with diarrhea. One time she didn't make it, and I had her *and* the floor to clean up. If she had wanted to create an unmistakable association between herself and a paranormal event, she had chosen the manifestation very well! I was delighted. The spirit obviously doesn't lose its sense of humor "on the other side."

The next morning, the boys and I talked over what I had witnessed. Danny allowed that he wouldn't mind my coming back to him, but he'd prefer me not to make any noise in the process. He suggested I just leave a cup of coffee sitting around somewhere as I was habitually prone to do and then forget where it was. Later that day, I had him take a pitcher of water into my bathroom and pour from it into the toilet bowl at sporadic intervals while I sat on my bed. The sound was identical to that which I had heard in the night.

A few weeks afterwards when Anamary's social worker came by to see how I was making it, we discussed what had happened. She had no trouble at all accepting the phenomena as Anamary's attempts to confirm her continuing spiritual presence in our lives. It was the first account she had heard involving actual material proof of contact by the deceased, but working as she did with families of elderly clients, who often died, she had been told many, many times by surviving kinfolk of their overwhelming sense of such a presence.

I have since pondered the enigma of the corresponding dates of the respective phenomena, believing somehow that they were not randomly chosen. If one applies the methods used in numerology, which traces its history to Hebrew (and depending upon the authority cited, possibly beyond to Chaldean) and the Kabbalah, an interesting result is obtained. Adding the numerical order of the months, February and March, yields the number five. So do both dates of the fourteenth, adding one and four. Five is the value in Hebrew of the letter *hey*, which, according to Lawrence Kushner, author of *The Book of Letters: A Mystical Alef-bait*, is associated with "I am present" or "Here am I."

If one adds together the three fives and then the one and five of the sum fifteen—the normal divinatory procedure in numerology (or the Kabbalistic *Gematria*)—the result is six, or the letter *vav*, the "symbol of completion, redemption and transformation" (from *The Wisdom of the Hebrew Alphabet* by Rabbi Michael L. Munk). Pure accident? Maybe, but then, maybe not.

It is also fascinating to note that *tes*, the first letter of the number fifteen, *tes vav*—Hebrew reads from right to left—has to do with water and is associated with the word *mud*. Mud itself, as discussed in *A Dictionary of Symbols*, stands for "the union of the purely receptive principle (earth) and the power of transition and transformation (water)." The fact that the rock fell when it was raining, embedding itself in the mud, and that the second manifestation also involved water could have some hidden meaning as well—perhaps that water is essential to unlocking the rock's dormant energy, if the psychic was right about its potential. It is of further interest that in *The Magus of Strovolos*, Kyriacos C. Markides mentions being told by Spyros Sathi (called "Daskalos") that water is the dominant element on the psychic planes. Whether anything is to be made from the additional fact that February 14 of 1983 corresponded to the equivalent of my birth date in the Hebrew calendar—*Rosh Chodesh* of *Adar* (the new moon, or first day of that month)—beyond, perhaps, an example of Jung's "synchronicities," far exceeds the limits of my comprehension to imagine.

The objection some might pose regarding Anamary's unfamiliarity with such features of the occult during life is not necessarily relevant. Physicists are establishing with more and more certainty that the physical and the metaphysical overlap and have as a common denominator certain mathematical characteristics. Words, numbers, colors, musical tones—everything vibrates to a given law yet to be enunciated definitely, but it is all there just the same. In his fascinating book *Hyperspace: A Scientific Odyssey Through Parallel Universes, Time Warps, and the Tenth Dimension*, physicist Michio Kaku reveals that attempts by scientists to reconcile quantum mechanics with general relativity produce mathematical formulae from which the numbers ten and twenty-six keep falling out almost like magic. What he does not go ahead to mention—and probably doesn't know—is that ten is the number of *Sephirot* constituting the Kabbalistic Tree of Life, or the emanations of the Godhead. Twenty-six is the numerical sum of the letter values in the name of God—*yud, hey, vav, hey*, or the more familiar YHVH in English. These correspondences have exciting and profound implications. It may not have been a matter of intention on Anamary's part that circumstances involving the rock and the sound of water splashing can be interpreted mystically. Rather, it might have been no more than an unavoidable concurrence with cosmic law.

Whatever the explanation, to believe that the soul is forever—or even temporarily—locked into the narrow scope of understanding its mental counterpart enjoyed on our material plane surely sells very short the prospects of eternity! It does not stretch credulity any further to believe Anamary had access to information essential to carrying out the full import of the message she wanted to convey than to believe she was actually capable of conveying it at all, and there's no doubt in my mind that she overtly and consciously did this very thing.

Mother had no doubts either when I called her about what had transpired. She returned to Oregon on Mother's Day with something obviously wrong with her. Debilitated by the physical and mental strain of the past several months, I had resigned my teaching position at the end of the winter term, feeling I couldn't do justice to my students in that condition. In a way I had not anticipated, the decision was extremely fortuitous. Mother choked on her food so frequently it was alarming, but she stubbornly refused to see a doctor. I finally couldn't stand it anymore, made a medical appointment for her, and announced that she was going to keep it.

CHAPTER THIRTEEN

There are times when everything seems to stop, when the brain freezes and, unmoved and unmoving, we sit like mannequins in a shop window, staring blindly through a glass panel beyond which the world continues to function without relevance to our isolation. The doctor spoke again across the gulf of my numbness, and I knew he was waiting for a reply.

"That's what I would do if it were my mother," he urged.

But it isn't, I thought; *it's mine.* Mine who had malignant tumor on her esophagus that all but closed it completely, leaving her only an eleven-millimeter opening for the passage of food. Without immediate treatment, that too would soon be blocked off and she would literally starve. This, he was saying, is just one of those things the elderly are prone to get if they outlive everything else. *That's nice to know!* I mused sardonically and wondered with Mark Twain what's wrong with thunderbolts, not so much because they're cheaper than forty-day and forty-night downpours, but because they're so blissfully sudden and therefore relatively painless. Cancer was the one thing Mother had always had the greatest dread of ever getting. Maybe that's the way it works, sort of the reverse psychology someone told me prevails in prison: find out what the inmates don't want and give them lots of it.

The doctor did not recommend surgery for Mother at her age, but hadn't Anamary survived it older than that? Why leave this up to me? Radiation therapy could halt the tumor's growth, but wouldn't that be hard on her too? Was he absolutely sure that's what he would choose for his own mother? He was sure, and this is finally what persuaded me to go along with his judgment. Because I did, Mother concurred as well when we went back into the examining room to tell her what she had already guessed. A treatment schedule was set up which would continue for the next three months, and we went home in the presence of an almost tangible awareness that made three an uncomfortable crowd. It was always *there*, intrusive as an unwelcome guest who denudes the pantry and eavesdrops at keyholes, depleting reserves and inhibiting normal conversation.

I had married again, but my husband was away, and then Danny left to spend part of his summer vacation with his father in California. Mother and I were left alone with our phantom companion. Charles had moved in with a friend and was reveling in the freedom of independence. Gradually we were able to talk candidly about her illness, about mistakes both of us had made and what they had taught us. Mother regretted ever having thought of sickness as being a kind of punishment for one's sins, for she found nothing in her past that would have merited cancer. It was the perennial conundrum posed by Job and answered in *Ecclesiastes*: "... time and chance happeneth ... to all." That is the best answer Western religion has to offer the suffering righteous.

The summer wore on. Danny returned home, and so did my husband, Roberto. Mother was still on her feet and in charge of doing dishes, but she grew steadily weaker. I was caught in the middle like the hub of a wheel on which all the spokes depend but without relating to one another. The best I could do to meet the disparate demands on me never seemed good enough, and in the aftermath of my hemorrhaging episode, when I was afraid to exert myself even minimally lest the bleeding start again, my sense of inadequacy was overwhelming. During that frightening period, Mother had been physically unable to help and merely suffered more because of her frustration. Only Danny had stood by me loyally. He came into the living room one night after everyone else had gone to bed and said, "I can't stand it anymore. I'm sleeping in here." He made himself a pallet on the floor beside me to be available if I needed anything and just to be near. I had remained on the sofa so as not to disturb my husband with my sudden eruptions of blood.

One evening Robert announced that he was going for a walk. I said I would come along, for I badly needed some fresh air and a change of scenery, however slight, and wanted his company besides. Nothing doing. He resented the proposed invasion of his privacy—probably he was on his way to obtain dope. Something snapped. Some last fragile thread of will, and therefore sanity, broke. That night I took a handful of Dalmane and drank most of a fifth of bourbon, for I was physically and emotionally exhausted and craved rest in any form it would take. Nothing else mattered anymore.

Before dropping into bed, I called Bruce in Wisconsin to say that if I didn't wake up, it was not his or anyone else's fault, that I loved them all but was just at the end of my rope. I knew nothing more until I awoke the next morning in the emergency room of the local hospital. A nurse asked how much I remembered. Only a dim recollection of vomiting. Bruce, I was told, had called the Sheriff's office from Madison and asked that deputies be sent to my apartment and had continued phoning during the night to inquire about my condition.

I was further told that when they questioned me about what I had done, I merely retorted, "I'm so tired, I don't care if I live or die." Now, however, I only wanted to go home. The nurse disappeared through the curtain of my cubicle, and the doctor appeared followed by a police officer. The doctor upbraided me about what I had done and said I could have wreaked some very serious damage on myself. Then he left, and I prepared to leave.

No such luck. The officer stopped me.

"I'm sorry," he said, "but I'll have to take you to the State Hospital."

"Why?" I protested. "I'm okay now. I need to go home!"

"It's regulation," he explained. "You're on a police hold because you tried to kill yourself."

"It was a stupid mistake," I confessed, "but I have to go home now. I'm needed."

But there was no way to circumvent the law. Wearing only a thin nightgown under a paper "robe" and with paper "slippers" on my feet, I was taken to OSH and left in a ward full of mentally ill patients, many of whom treated me to various manifestations of such curiosity as they were capable of expressing. I felt sick and colder than I could ever remember being in my entire life. When an aide came through, I asked how I could go about being released. I would first have to have a recommendation from the County pre-release counselor. Who was that, and how could I contact that person?

My heart leapt up when I heard the woman's name, for she had been Anamary's social worker before taking her new job with the Mental Health Division. Would someone call her? No. I must do that myself on the pay phone in the ward, but just incidentally, she was off for the weekend and could not be reached. The sundry impulses that popped into my mind would have earned me extended residence in my current prison. The only safe alternative was to nag, and nag I did. This produced additional information: someone else was on call for her, and I was given his number.

When I finally got through to him and explained the situation, he said he would talk to his colleague and get back to me. In the meantime, I was frantic. I knew that, inadequate as I was, my family had no one else to depend on but me. I had been insufferably selfish in trying to escape from my responsibilities.

I did not hear from the psychologist directly, but at length I was taken into a screening session with a resident—or perhaps consulting—psychiatrist and the staff of that wing. The doctor didn't want to let me go on the assumption that if circumstances at home did not change, I would try the same thing again and possibly succeed. I assured him I would not. He reluctant signed my release at last on the condition that I undergo therapy with a counselor of my choice. The former social worker didn't normally take on private clients, but she made an exception for me. I accepted that arrangement and went home, contrite and apologetic. The first day I walked into her office, she greeted me with "The surprising thing is that you waited so long. I expected this months ago." She could do nothing to alleviate my problems, but she listened patiently as I described them. That was something at least.

Mother contracted pneumonia again, and when she came home that time, we got a hospital bed to facilitate her care, for she was failing rapidly. Her birthday that year, the twenty-fourth of November, fell on Thanksgiving. We had turkey and a lovely cake, but she could only look at them and drink the shake I prepared in a blender. She was ninety-three and wondered if she would make it till Christmas. Roberto asked her to come back to him, since I had Anamary. She laughed her old quick laugh and said she would if she could.

Robert was complicating things beyond measure. I had naively believed his drug addiction to be in permanent remission when I married him, but I was soon to learn otherwise. He had a swing-shift job from which he arrived home around two o'clock in the morning. Mother slept very lightly, and she reported to me that he crept into her room each time he got in and drank her morphine before going to bed. I confronted him, but he denied doing any such thing, blaming her suspicions on the addled brain of a senile and terminally ill old woman. I knew my mother better than that. Senile she was not, and I set a trap.

We kept just four ounces of the medication in a plastic container by Mother's bed for her convenience, and I put away the larger bottle from the pharmacy. The solution was blue, precisely the color of Windex. Using that as my base, therefore, I made up a substitute, adding a bit of cherry flavoring and just a tad of rubbing alcohol for the necessary tang. I had no idea what effect it would have on the thief, but I frankly didn't much care at that point. Taking her and Danny into my confidence, I left it by her bed in the accustomed container.

Roberto was still asleep when I got up the next morning. Danny greeted me with a grin.

"Roberto was up earlier and said he was sick," Danny volunteered. I checked the erzatz morphine. Half of it was gone.

"Good!" I exclaimed. "We'll see what the gentleman has to say now!"

The "gentleman" didn't have a lot he could say. He did claim that he had obtained permission from Mother to use her morphine for pain (and he always managed to have pain somewhere). Perhaps he had asked for some once or twice when he actually worked up the nerve, but it had not been a *carte blanche* kind of authorization. The marriage was destined to deteriorate from then on, but I had no time to brood about it, for as Mother became more and more bedridden, I left her side only when it was absolutely necessary. One day she began talking to me about her "black angels."

"I call them that," she explained. "I don't know what they really are."

At first I thought she had read something in the newspaper about a group of Black teenagers in Portland who had banded together to help the elderly in their neighborhoods and do good deeds in general, but then I suddenly realized this was something altogether different.

"There are four of them," she was telling me. "I call them my 'black angels' because they wear black robes, but they have wreaths of yellow chrysanthemums on their chests."

Chrysanthemums are the flower for November, and they were Mother's favorites. I was listening intently now. She went on.

"The last time they were here," she said, "they put up a canopy and held some kind of a service, and then they folded it and left." I thought immediately of a graveside ceremony.

"I hope you're here the next time they come," she continued. So did I.

Within days, I returned from shopping one afternoon and went in to see about her and to show her what I had bought. She had always said that she wanted to be buried in something warm because she anticipated "feeling cold," having always been very cold-natured. It was a standard joke in the family that she only pulled off her sweater on the Fourth of July. I had found a nice woolen suit of a rich brown color, and she approved heartily.

"You just missed them!" she said when I had put everything away and sat down by her bed.

"Who?" I asked, thinking it was probably one of our neighbors.

"The black angels," she told me.

"What happened this time?" I prodded.

I was not merely humoring a dying woman's delusions. I believed something out of the ordinary had taken place.

"They just stood around my bed," she answered. "I asked the one who seems to be the leader when they plan to be back, for I want you to see them!"

"What did he say?" I asked.

"Well, that was the curious part," she replied. "He didn't say anything. He just held out his thumb to me. The nail was half white and half black." She indicated a line running vertically down the middle of her own round thumbnail. "I wondered if they all had nails like that!" she continued.

It didn't make any sense to either of us, though it had clearly been offered as an answer to her question. The four messengers (if that is what they were) had left without further ado and were not to return again—not so that I learned about it from her, at least.

One of Mother's fondest wishes was to go back to Missouri to visit relatives there. It was not possible, either from the standpoint of her condition or our financial straits. Her longing weighed on my heart. In the meantime, not able to afford a Christmas tree and lacking the spirit to put one up as well, I strung lights around her window and hung baubles from the wire, attaching evergreen boughs purloined from nearby trees. It was a feeble gesture to cheer things up, but the effect was more poignant than nothing at all would have been.

Along about the same time, I started noticing something strange. Dead of winter notwithstanding, a frog began croaking under Mother's window every night. I scarcely believed in "omens," but this unseasonable minstrel sent an unpleasant tingle down my spine. There was no stream near us nor even a pond that I knew anything about. In any event, the creature should have been hibernating somewhere, for there were certainly no insects around for him to eat at that time of year. I had heard of dogs howling and owls hooting as harbingers of death, but frogs croaking? This was not only eerie but absurd!

As I sat by Mother's side one evening, she began to talk to family members both long and recently dead, looking from one to another, addressing them specifically by name and waiting for replies. Anamary was there, as I would have expected. In the course of her "conversation," the scenario unfolded: we had driven to Missouri, and our car had broken down. Charles and some of the other fellows were working on it. She related why we had moved to Oregon, quite accurately, and missing Danny, turned to include me in her fantasy.

"Where's Danny?" she asked.

"He's spending the night with Mike," I reminded her, as indeed he was.

"Oh, that's right," she said, turning back to account to her audience for his absence.

One thing in particular intrigued me. She saw her aunt Lizzie, dead long before I was born, and said, "I know you're Aunt Lizzie, but you don't look like her! Your hair's not right!" Why, if this was nothing but hallucination, didn't she see the woman exactly as she remembered her? Everyone else apparently looked the same. Evidence has been documented that disembodied spirits can assume the appearance of any age they wish. It made me wonder.

The "reunion" continued until it was obvious that Mother was becoming very weary and her voice was giving out. I manipulated the controls on her bed so that it moved and told her the car was fixed now, we could go home. She accepted this as a natural consequence, said her goodbyes, and took my hand."

"Hang on tight," she said, "and let's go to sleep."

Our roles reversed now, I clasped the wasted hand she tendered. How many dishes had it washed, how many pieces of clothing had it scrubbed, how many tears had it dried, how many rips had it mended, how many meals had it prepared? No Madame Bovary's, this, with her licentious excesses. This was the hand of the biblical Martha, who had served her God in a practical way, no less essential in its attention to the real world than Mary's pursuit of the supernal. Mother went to sleep, peacefully it seemed. The next morning as I helped her with her toilet, she complained of being tired.

"But no wonder!" she exclaimed. "We drove all the way to Missouri and back yesterday!"

Delighted that she remembered and hoping the illusion would now sustain her, I went along with it wholeheartedly, for there was an all too familiar look on her face that morning. I had noted it on Anamary's just before she lapsed into her coma. It is the look of impending death, fleeting but unforgettable. It cannot be described, only experienced, but as nearly as words will serve, it is the face of a very young child. There is a dramatically sudden softening of the features, and the eyes bespeak a kind of innocence that at once portrays complete trust and total dependence. It is otherworldly in its seeming oblivion to present realities. There is something searching about it, but with a paradoxically resigned, yet wistful, blindness. It passes as suddenly as it comes, and the face resumes its former appearance.

There was other evidence that the end was not far off. Mother was astounded that her hand would go through solid objects and called me to witness what she assumed I could see as well as she. I took this to be an indication that her spirit somehow detached itself but still registered its behavior through the normal channels of perception. She also had a typically spontaneous resurgence of energy one day soon. Holding to the wall to steady herself, she walked alone to the living room, sat there awhile and walked back to bed again, first rearranging things on the top of her bureau. I knew this must have caused terrible pain, for I could no longer even turn her in bed without causing grimaces of agony. Her courage was heartbreaking. It is always the brave who earn our tears. I still remember a four-year-old boy brought to the St. Louis

Children's Hospital Emergency Room, where I worked one summer as an undergraduate student. He had a compound fracture of one arm, but not a whimper did he make. I therefore wanted to cry for him. Cowards do their own whining.

Shortly after this, I again had a difficult decision to make: I couldn't bear to hurt Mother anymore with my necessary ministrations. Besides, she was not taking in enough nourishment. I wanted someone to tell me what to do, to take the responsibility off my shoulders, to say, "This is best, and you are exonerated of the consequences." *Let this cup pass from me!* How real and human that cry! I was at least in good company.

The compulsion to alleviate immediate suffering prevailed, and I sent Mother to the hospital, wrapping her up as warmly as I could against the flakes of snow that drifted down on her as she was carried to the ambulance. Both of us knew she would not come back. In the silent emptiness she left behind, I leaned my head against the door of her room and sobbed for a long time—for all I should have said that I didn't say; for all that I could not call back to do over; for love that defies expression because we perversely defy love, imagining it a weakness in ourselves instead of strength; for bringing her to a strange place to die among strangers.

The next day she seemed better, but it was a tenuous improvement. The doctor had humanely ordered "as much morphine as she [needed]," having determined by X-ray that two of her vertebrae had completely disintegrated. How she had stood to move at all was beyond his comprehension.

That evening, to my surprise and chagrin, Roberto prepared to leave with the truck to play bridge. I asked him not to go, but he countered with a heated tirade on the unthinkable discourtesy of canceling out on a committed bridge partner. Forget the offense to a marital partner. No more than half an hour after he left, a nurse called from the hospital saying Mother's breathing was very labored and perhaps I should come at once. A neighbor kindly gave me a ride, and I went braced for the inevitable.

The night dragged on endlessly. Mother's hand, in mine, burned with fever, and her body shook violently. Why did it have to be so hard? Why couldn't she, like many, have slipped away quietly in the peaceful unawareness of natural slumber? The poet was a fool who counseled "Do not go gently into that good night." I felt angry and bitter. Sometime early in the morning, I laid my head down on her bed, not meaning to sleep, but I roused with a start when a nurse touched my shoulder lightly.

"Mama's gone now," she said and took me in her arms. "Thank you for being here with her."

But I shouldn't have been sleeping, I thought, and remembered another very human cry. *Could you not watch with me one hour?* Ah, why can the flesh not be as strong as the spirit is willing? I was led out of the room to take care of routine details and call home to be picked up. It was shortly after 7:00 a.m. on Christmas Eve. She had almost made it to Christmas. I stood looking at a small courtyard below, its landscaping features obliterated in mounds and hollows of snow that still fell aimlessly, soundlessly. It was comforting somehow in its statement of unmarred quiescence.

What a beautiful time to die! I mused. Then I remembered. That day was her wedding anniversary.

There were the usual duties to perform: calls to make, arrangements to finalize. I couldn't go back with her to Missouri as I had with Anamary. There wasn't enough money for the trip, but the same friend would be there to carry out my wishes. This eulogy had been prepared in advance too, with the same loving concern for a fitting tribute that would stress the dignity of life and the value of selfless devotion to others.

That night, two things came to my attention that were to make lasting impressions. The frog was silent for the first time in weeks and was not heard from again. The other discovery was much more profound in its implications. My bed stood under a high window whose drapes were always closed, since it faced the street. Never before had I done such a thing, nor had I any purpose in mind when I did it then, but on an irrepressible impulse, I pulled the curtain aside and looked out preliminary to getting into bed. There, directly in my line of vision, was the moon—exactly at the half: half black, half white.

"Oh, my God!" I gasped, clutching the windowsill.

The mysterious "black angel" had been telling my mother that she would die when the moon's phases reached the half—that he and his companions would return for her then. And they did, right on schedule.

CHAPTER FOURTEEN

Danny was in California with his father for the winter break from school. Wanting simply to be alone, I insisted that Roberto leave as well and spend the holidays with his family in Portland. Because he had been of no support to me when I desperately needed it, anything he might have done in the immediate wake of Mother's death would have been too little, too late. I wanted the freedom to adjust at my own pace and in my own way without having to deal with resentment or mundane routine.

The first thing I did the day after Christmas was to buy an enormous album and drag out a huge box of photographs I had kept adding to over the years with the usual good intentions. Sitting in the floor with these scattered all around me, I spent a whole night arranging them by family and chronology. It was probably the most therapeutic thing I could have done. My "reunion" was not quite so animated as Mother's had been, but it served to evoke many pleasant memories. My personal loss at that point was secondary to the overwhelming relief I felt that Mother was no longer suffering.

By the time Roberto returned, I was much restored in mind and body and ready to take on whatever challenges the marriage presented, still hoping it could be salvaged under the more normal conditions that then obtained, but I had yet to take a full measure of my adversary—if, indeed, the complete horror of drug addiction can ever be totally comprehended. Drugs are more insidious than alcohol as agents of personal destruction and social disorder. Their effects are more unpredictable, and their use is not accompanied by the telltale warning to others that alcohol at least provides on the breath. The financial drain they create is only one of the myriad evils of the nightmare that envelopes the addict and everyone his habit touches. It was that which would fulfill Roberto's half-jesting request of Mother that she come back to him.

Because it was the end of the month, my "cash flow" had dwindled to less than a trickle: in a word, drought had set in. I had one twenty-dollar bill left to buy such staples as bread and milk, but Roberto's demands for money became so insistent that I finally gave it to him. It was not enough. There is no such thing as "enough money" in an addict's frame of reference. He blew up. I was working in the kitchen at the time, and, exasperated, I asked if it meant nothing to him to have a roof over his head.

Just as I bent to pick up something from the floor, he struck at me, catching me completely by surprise. The blow fell across the right side of my face. I had never before been hit by a man, and never in anger by anyone or in the face. I had no intention of beginning to countenance such abuse at that stage of the game. I came up livid, telling him to pack his things immediately and get out. Much subdued, he tried to pass the incident off lightly, but I threw his clothes into a bag and, making it clear he would either leave with me or with the police, I took him to the bus depot and left him there.

It was a while before I returned home, for I first went to Charles' apartment to sob out my rage, having always been one of those unfortunate people who cry when they're angry, making it appear that they're merely indulging in self-pity. No sooner had I gotten back home than the phone rang, and it was Roberto asking if he could return just temporarily until he could make some other living arrangements.

My instincts, which I have always violated to my sorrow, impelled me to say no, and I did. He seemed genuinely contrite, however, and I relented enough to say I would come discuss it with him. Still angry but purged, at least, of my homicidal inclinations, I drove back to the bus station calm and collected, but resistant to any pleas for reconciliation. He was, admittedly, in a considerable bind, and my early indoctrination in respect to turning the other cheek and going the extra mile finally triumphed over my indignation, so we returned home together with the understanding that within a week or so, he would leave voluntarily.

Roberto slept late the next morning and did not make an appearance until about 11:30 when a friend left who had dropped by to take care of some business pertaining to an organization on whose board we both served. As soon as she was gone, he came into the living room requesting that I come look at the bed. This was the same one that stood under the window facing the street. He had left a crack of the sliding pane standing open, no wider than two inches at the most. It would not have admitted an adult fist and was much too high to be reached by a child. In addition, the drapes were still closed. Yet what had wakened him amounted to a heaped-up double handful of dirt and bark dust that had been dumped directly on his face. Had it merely been thrown at the window, it wouldn't have come through or under the drapes in such a way as to be concentrated in one place. It was still lying on the pillow on either side of where his head had lain. I had to remove the sheet from the bed, take it outside and shake it. In addition, Roberto's right cheek was red and swollen—so much so that he was alarmed about a possible infection.

I regarded him in thoughtful silence.

"You don't have an infection," I said. "You may recall that *my* cheek hurt pretty badly and turned red yesterday. I think we can safely assume that you've just been paid a visit by my mother!"

Within a couple of hours, the redness and swelling in his face were gone without a trace. Whether Mother had come back to wreak such vengeance as she could on him—and I firmly believe she did—he was sufficiently convinced of it that his behavior was exemplary until he left. I told gave an account of this to an old neighbor when I went back to Missouri the following summer to visit Mother's grave and select a stone for Anamary's. I had scarcely finished speaking when she exclaimed, "Your mother hit him!" Evelyn Hagans never struck me as being the impressionable type. She was a sophisticated and high cultured woman in her seventies then whom I would have judged to be very conservative, in fact. She went on to tell me her own experience of many years before.

Her husband John, whom I remember fondly, died suddenly and very unexpectedly of a heart attack. His death left her devastated. For weeks she had uncontrollable bouts of weeping that drained her energy and interfered with normal activity. One morning, she related to me, she lay on her bed sobbing when she heard John's voice calling her name. She turned to look in the direction from which the sound came and saw him standing there in broad daylight as clearly as she had ever seen him before in the flesh.

"Don't carry on so, Evelyn!" he chided her. "Don't you realize I'm still here with you?"

So saying, he disappeared, but the event completely changed her attitude, and she was able to pick up her life and go on without further outbursts of unrestrained grief.

I have never understood why so many people profess fear of such apparitions. Having had no reason to be afraid of John in life, Evelyn would have certainly had no reason to fear him as pure spirit. Many of these same people also profess to believe in the immortality of the soul; apparently they just want it to be immortal in some place safely distant from them! The invention of Heaven (or Sheol or Hades or whatever) was inevitable. There is a comfortable remoteness about such a place. But what if one's mother or father or husband or wife really hangs around after death watching everything one does? Sobering thought, isn't it? If this were generally accepted as fact, the effect on human behavior would be more salubrious than that which religion has ever been able to produce with all its promises of reward and threats of punishment.

While I would have been delighted to see Mother and Anamary—Dad too—I was not privileged to do so, unless it was really Anamary's presence in bed with me that night. There was another strange event, though, which both Danny and I witnessed. We were sitting in the living room one afternoon reading when a music box on the piano began to play of its own accord. I had bought it for my father in New York years before, and as far as anyone knew, it was broken. We had not been able to get it to work for quite some time, but because of its sentimental value, I still kept in out in sight. Its tune was one of Mozart's sonatas, and it normally ran no longer than five minutes before winding down. Startled by its sudden intrusion into the silence, I glanced at the clock sitting beside it. That time it played for twenty minutes! Even if a frozen gear had slipped, releasing the mechanical apparatus in some natural fashion, it would have been technically impossible for it to run that long. There seemed to be no logical explanation but a supernatural one. Whoever—or whatever—was responsible, the effect was one of solace and joy. Besides, the music box was restored, and it functioned properly from then on to the very present.

It was not until the next Mother's Day that grief caught up with me. It was the first one I had spent without a mother, and I completely fell apart. Even anti-depressants were ineffectual. Like Evelyn Hagans, I couldn't seem to stop crying. It was not safe to go out in public, for I might break down anywhere, anytime. This went on until I was at the end of my wits. Then one night I had a dream in which Mother appeared to me and, much like John Hagans had done to his wife, upbraided me.

"Don't worry," she said, "about any unhappiness you feel you might have caused me. It will more than be compensated by for what your own children will put you through."

I awoke pensive but no longer sorrowing. She had correctly identified the real source of my disconsolation. There was more of guilt than grief about it.

She was right, of course. Everything one does gets back to him sometime, one way or another. "What goes around comes around," as the subculture aphorism puts it. Cause and effect create an ongoing chain of events which we forge ourselves, just as old Marley told Scrooge. The links are not broken at death. They bind us to another life and another opportunity to fashion them delicately of gold refined in the crucible of love rather than burdensome iron wrought with spite and narrow self-interest. When we learn how to do that, then—and only then—can we detach ourselves *if we wish*—and really be free.

CHAPTER FIFTEEN

For many years—at least thirty—people who knew me well kept saying that I owed it to the world to write. I'm not convinced that the world will agree with them, but I am sure why it has taken me until now to comply with pressures they brought to bear.

As I searched for some coherence to my life, I realized that sooner or later I came to question every new "answer" I found, in part or in whole. Every time I felt compelled to set down my observations, something held me back—some "still, small voice" that warned me to wait awhile for fear I would have to look back years later upon public testimony to nothing but my own ignorance. One wishes that many writers in print would have had similar inhibitions, for I taught long enough to be familiar with the common notion that the written word is the *last* word—that if it weren't true, it wouldn't be in print. Nothing could be more fallacious.

Insofar as language is capable of recapitulating experience, everything I have related in *A For White Roses* is true; however, interpretation of actual fact is personal and therefore always susceptible of error. I recall an incident years ago in Milwaukee, where the family was driving along Lake Michigan. It was a glorious day of blues and golds. I was ecstatic about the gemlike green running through the lake's blue depths and kept urging Danny and his father to look.

"I don't see any green!" young Danny insisted.

"There! Right there!" I said, pointing. His gaze followed my finger.

"There isn't any green," he argued stubbornly.

I became incensed. Nobody was going to tell me I didn't see what I was seeing! To accentuate my own obstinancy, I jerked off my sunglasses for more direct eye contact with my antagonist. Lo and behold! The green disappeared! It had been visible only through the polarized lenses. We had both been right and both been wrong. That's the way perception is, and I learned an enduring lesson from this one, otherwise insignificant, event. A great deal of blood has been shed throughout history over differences just as trifling and just as predicated upon imperfect perception.

If my views seem to reflect an undertow of ambivalence running through my life, pulling me away from intended progress towards a safe harbor of certain conviction, it is because, quite simply, it's really present as a force to be reckoned with. It is evident, for example, that I deeply resent the attitude that adoption is a facile solution to the problem of unwanted pregnancy, yet admittedly, with the benefit of hindsight I can honestly say I am glad to have been adopted. Circumstances, as it's said, alter cases. A psychic told me once that I would have been an alien anyplace, even with my birth mother. She was probably right.

There are those, adopted or otherwise, whose longing to fit into an established order will always be futile. It seldom appears to them that they are fortunate by virtue of this, and many choose responses to it that brand them as "misfits," becoming outlaws or rebels or recluses or merely eccentrics, tolerated within certain limits but always vaguely distrusted. If they have within them the qualities essential to greatness, they blaze trails through the jungle of man's ignorance, often losing their lives as a consequence. Sometimes the jungle closes in again, and the paths must be reclaimed by others, who invariably think themselves the first to penetrate their particular wilderness. And so it goes on.

Some inroads remain open, however, so thoroughly have the barriers to knowledge in their course been rooted out. Even these are not immune to changes by—what shall we call them?—civil engineers, perhaps: early travelers who venture along them, erecting signs for those who follow. Then the trouble begins. Perhaps the path looks too dangerous to accommodate heavy traffic, and barricades are erected reading "Keep Out—Trespassers Will Be Prosecuted." Or perhaps a toll gate is set up limiting access to a privileged class willing and able to pay dearly for its use. Or, yet again, perhaps it's so attractive that "One Way" signs are posted, precluding a later change of direction.

Such is the progress of "civilization" and all it embraces, from religion to medicine, from technology to quantum physics. In the meanwhile, we are still engulfed by the jungle, so immeasurable in its dimensions that one of our most lasting misconceptions is the extent of our remaining ignorance.

When I taught high-school English back in the 60s and early 70s, I was appalled by the assembly-line approach to education. There was no place in it for the questioning mind, the skeptic, the creative visionary. If it was true in the public-school system, how much more is it true of parochial schools with particular axes to grind and private theories to defend. This, of course, is what Mother recognized and why she took me out of Immaculate Conception when she did. My mind was about to be set in concrete at a time when I had not yet developed the tools for critical analysis of the mould into which it was being poured. In the long run, even though she regretted the emotional trauma her decision inflicted, she made the right one, and I have come to forgive her with all my heart.

If the Catholic school was conservative in its approach to disseminating knowledge, it stood as a bastion of academic freedom compared to more fundamentalist religious institutions. Ironically, it was Jewish Kabbalists and the Christian mystics who emulated them that kept inquiry alive as a flickering candle in the gloom of the Dark Ages. Inevitably, though, when a flame ignites a conflagration that lights up more of the night than narrow concepts can accommodate, then the reverse process begins: shades are drawn against the brightness, and walls are built to protect the candle, sacred only because it has burned so long, not because of what it revealed.

A vast majority of Westerners still reject the mounting evidence that refutes much of their religious dogma in terms of man and his relationship to the cosmos, even though it suggests a great deal more "justice and mercy" than prevailing creeds allow for. When I related my experience with what I call the "Anamary rock" to an old high-school friend, she cut me off with a note of alarm in her voice.

"I don't believe in all that!" she hurried to exclaim. "I believe in God and Jesus!"

Of what was she afraid? Was her faith in God so shaky that a rock falling out of the sky could threaten it? Does that say much for God?

I have also heard an Orthodox Jewish rabbi disparage belief in reincarnation even as he held in his very hand the prayer book (*siddur*) containing the "Prayer Before Retiring at Night" that reads

> Master of the Universe! I hereby forgive anyone who has angered me, either physically or financially, against my honor or anything else that is mine, whether accidentally or intentionally, inadvertently or deliberately, by speech or by deed, *in this incarnation or in any other*. . . . [Emphasis mine]

Of what was he afraid? Though it is seldom known among non-Jews, the Chassidic Jewish sects, basing their beliefs and practices on the ancient Oral Tradition also advanced by the biblical Pharisees, accept reincarnation as a given.

If I have seemed inconsistent in my attitude concerning religion, quoting isolated Scripture but deriding its reputation for infallibility overall, longing for the trappings of tradition but rejecting the strictures they impose, I but reflect the agony of the ages. Our yearning toward the order implicit in formal worship and the pomp explicit in its rituals is no more than a universal impulse to impose comprehensible limitations and decorative trimming on the seeming chaos of *Infinite Possibility*, which I believe God to be. Although the urge itself is reflective of a pattern in "the One, the All," the tapestry of its design still eludes our vision except for a tiny stitch here and there.

Even saints grow restive, forced too long to kneel. Equilibrium is inimical to Life—Life in its totality, whatever that is. Stasis and growth are mutually exclusive, and anyone who seeks to thwart the natural processes of evolution in all spheres of existence, spiritual as well as material, impedes the progress it is man's purpose, not only to experience, but to promote. The ritualistic expression of an idea frozen in time thousands of years ago—if it is not what we might call "generic"—is as useless to our spiritual development now as medieval armor would be in atomic-age warfare.

In many ways, collective Man is the orphan of the Universe. His striving to achieve meaning and to identify his origins is closely analogous to that of the adopted child. Until such time as he comes face to face with the nature of reality, he may, as I did, imagine any background he pleases and treat it as fact. If I was interested in medicine, my father had certainly been a doctor; if music, my mother had certainly been a musician. The images changed to fit my changing aspirations and emotional needs. So, too, has Man continued throughout history to create a spiritual and biological *vita* compatible with the demands of his changing social and geographical milieu.

The problem arises when these are no longer complementary, for it is difficult to relinquish our fantasies if we have based our concept of self upon their supposed authenticity. At no time in history has this been more evident than it is now when environmental and social forces are playing havoc with old concepts of identity. Where individual egos have fused to become the mass ego of the herd, there is nothing to stop the inevitable mindless stampede of blind will towards survival of the group as a distinct entity, regardless of what destruction ensues or how many of its own members are sacrificed in the mad dash for a permanent presence in what is really an impermanent world.

I could well have returned from Michigan after meeting my sister completely devastated by the revealed absence of any extraordinary heritage with which to corroborate and vindicate, as it were, the potentials already evident early in my childhood. For a very long time, I had relied—almost apologetically—on that imaginary source for the talents that tended to intimidate and even alienate those whose affections I craved. Granted that my paternal history is still shrouded in mystery, my disillusionment at last gave me the freedom to be myself and to assume sole responsibility for all that entails, both for good and for ill. It was a kind of epiphany, as sobering in its implications as it was unburdening. The upshot of the whole catharsis that reached its climax in my husband's office that afternoon on returning from Michigan was, in a sense, learning who I *was* as well as who I *was not* and finally accepting both. From then on I could make choices quite independent of any preconceived obligation to be someone either more than or less than I really am. Without knowing it, I had come to accept *complete personal responsibility* in the framework of a just and moral Universe as understood in Hindu philosophy and explained beautifully by the idea of *karma*.

I am now, among other things, thankful for my perennial status as an "outsider." How very lucky I was! It is no accident, I'm sure, that I was destined to experience the lessons of this lifetime in that particular circumstance, for extrapolated to other facets of living, it has taught me that the true *self*, whose innate sense of being has not been obscured by the physical machinations of consciousness, resists—and rightly so—any attempt to confine it within the several cramped enclaves constructed from limited perceptions of the metaphysical.

I would try once more to "fit in," however, by embracing Judaism in its older and more mystical constructs, believing—as I still do—that there are some things of value to be gleaned from them, but again I found impediments to any actual condition of "belonging." History merely repeated itself. What I have discovered there is just enough suggestion of probable Truth to tantalize, but Truth so interwoven with patent nonsense that it cannot be extracted without violence either to one's integrity or to the fabric of which it is a part.

Something I determined long ago with respect to sexual behavior holds true all the way up the line: it is folly to send one's body into any situation where the heart does not go or to send one's heart into situations where the head does not go. Unless our choices can be endorsed by all three, they are *ipso facto* wrong, for we are all of a piece, more so than the ordinary person realizes or even wants to admit. To strike the perfect balance in this trinity of very real dimensions is the burden of humankind to accomplish, first individually and then collectively. Such a synthesis would, in and of itself, perhaps usher in that time of peace and well being so long awaited and so variously envisioned. My personal insight, again, merely echoes the ancient Hindu wisdom expressed in the *Katha Upanishad:* . . . "the Self is the Lord of the chariot, the body is verily the chariot; know that the soul is the charioteer, and emotion the reins."

The *Higher Self* is distinct from the *soul* in Eastern philosophy and is tantamount to a *god within.* The concept has been suppressed in Western religion, but it is there: "*I have said, Ye are gods, and all of you are children of the Most High*" (*Psalms* 82:6). Yet Jesus was accused of blasphemy for admitting he was the "*Son of the Blessed*" (*Mark* 15:16). Another expression of this same theme can be found in Schwaller de Lubicz's *The Egyptian Miracle: An Introduction to the Wisdom of the Temple* where he says, "Oneness of source, oneness of aim, oneness of function, form a solidarity that is the moral basis of superior man."

When I first began painting in 1972, I had a remarkable dream that was to plague me for a decade before a sudden turn in my life revealed its significance. In it, I was showing a friend a work I had done and was explaining to him why it was a masterpiece. Its title was *Dance of the Eternal Nightmare*, and in the dream I fully understood its relationship to the picture. When I awoke, however, the connection eluded me. Try hard as I might to recapture my discourse on it, I only drew a blank.

What *Dance* depicted was almost as bizarre as the name. Against a background of heavy, burgundy velvet drapery there stood a bed covered with a white counterpane embroidered with white, such as young girls once prepared for their hope chests. Standing on this in many length-wise rows were flowers of various kinds, some common and some rare, but all exquisitely beautiful and all swaying in precisely the same attitude as if to compelling ethereal music. At the foot of the bed stood an old-fashioned sea chest off whose curved lid there trailed strands of wet seaweed. When I was eventually able to put all the pieces together, this item would clinch for me the belief that I did, in fact, drown in a previous life. It is probably no mere coincidence that my first name—which I always hated and would not respond to—means "from the sea," a fact I discovered only recently.

At the time I had the dream, I had not given any serious thought to reincarnation, one way or the other. As the years went by, however, and I was drawn to examine carefully the persuasions advanced for supporting such a theory, I could not help but see the mysterious painting as a pictorial representation of that very process. I had a distinct funereal sense of the background drapery, since it reminded me of the typical backdrop for caskets provided by many mortuaries. Its color, moreover, combining blue and red, symbolizes innocence and passion, or spirituality and physical life blended together.

We *are* that combination in our earthly existences. Sometimes we live lives of a common garden variety and sometimes of exotic and rare specimens. Each has its unique place in the scheme of things, and each life, in its own way, has the potential for being beautiful, just as the flowers were in their suspended terpsichorean animation, redolent with a grace that in its duplication throughout could only result from harmony with a single implied rhythm.

They did not grow from the bed; rather, their stems were neatly and cleanly cut so that even in the full flush of radiant bloom, death was already an intrinsic part of the *programme*. They had been cut in some distant garden, not of the earth, where death is the piper that must be paid for life. The melody to which they danced is orchestrated on some level beyond both.

In spite of its macabre name, the tone of the painting was joyful, and in the dream I was incredibly happy and exhilarated by the fact that I had produced this thing of consummate loveliness and wisdom. Its tone seemed incompatible with the negative light shed on Man's fate by the title, however, and I was troubled by the dichotomy for a long time. It then occurred to me that a *nightmare* is, itself, a *dream*—a mere illusion not to be feared upon waking. Caught up in it, we see only the horror and not the total picture, which is one of great beauty. We will awake from physical existence to that Life in which what we have left behind will all seem like a bad dream.

The reason we remain as oblivious to the creative whole as a single blossom is to its role in the complete panorama of cosmic reality is that it is *too* obvious. We try to find it in the spectacular, the rare, the hidden, the "miraculous," but it is all around us, all the time—as well as *in* us.

In the Hindu legend of the monster *Kirttimukha*, "Face of Glory," the god *Shiva* creates him to get rid of yet another monster. Having done that, *Kirttimukha* is still hungry and, at *Shiva's* bidding, begins to devour himself. Is this not life consuming life in order to sustain life? Put another way, isn't it *Yahweh's* warning to Moses that no man can look upon the face of God and live? No man can live without dying, and God and Life are synonymous.

Almost like a sequel delayed until I had grasped the intended symbolism of *Dance*, a later dream involved another painting which I was showing to Anamary. It depicted a section of fencerow flanked by common weeds, stiffly dry and winter brown. Except for one patch of sunlight that fell aslant, the scene was plunged into dark umbers of somber shadow, but those weeds touched by the sun's rays were breathtaking in the splendor of their golden glow. The lowly, this suggests, if seen in the proper light (of Eternal Radiance) partakes as much of true beauty as the most highly prized product of greenhouse cultivation. The simplest life is as valuable as the most acclaimed—not only in its prime, but in death as well.

A still later dream projected upon the screen of my subconscious a condensed summary of my long quest. It was one of those spectator/participant dreams in which I watched myself trying on many formal dresses, none of which fit or suited my taste. Then I found one that was perfect. Under a long cape—again of burgundy velvet—swept back over my shoulders, I wore a shimmering gossamer gown embroidered from hem to neckline with a stylized but gorgeous Tree of Life, interestingly enough, a fig tree, often used in Christian art instead of the apple tree as being symbolic of the Tree of Knowledge and thus of both lust and fertility. Contrary to the traditional constructions placed upon sex and morality in Western religion, there seemed nothing indecent about the gown's transparency, for what it revealed was the Soul itself. In that mystical image probably lies the complete answer. The Soul takes on the garment of Life—the very fabric of which is woven from and embellished by Knowledge—and throws over this temporary attire the clock of mortality. It never ceases to shine through these habiliments, however, always remaining visible to the discerning eye.

The virginal white counterpane of the *Dance* dream, on a bed where "deflowering" normally takes place, is too obvious a symbol even to justify comment. In this setting we return again and again to physical form, thereby satisfying a desire that cannot be fulfilled in spirit—to mate, to merge, to create new life with its potential for greater and greater knowledge, *ad infinitum.* Could the spirit evolve without a physical matrix in which to experience what cannot otherwise be felt and learned? The answer is self-evident.

These—or similar—propositions have been advanced before in many ways by many others, both ancient and modern, notably Hindus and Buddhists. There is also a reference to Aztec philosophy that says poetically what my *Dance* dream said to me visually so long ago. It occurs in *Communion: A True Story* by Whitley Strieber. He discusses the Aztec concept of the God and Goddess of Duality and the impact of their harmonious union. "What is his flower? What is her song?" ask the philosophers, and they are told

The flowers sprout, they are fresh, they grow;
They open their blossoms,
And from within emerge the flowers of song;
Among men You scatter them, You send them.

My flowers shall not cease to live;
My songs shall never end;
I, a singer, intone them:
They become scattered, they are spread about.

The message is not often couched in poetry, but in prose works too esoteric and formidable for widespread appeal, more's the pity. What makes my personal experience worth sharing, therefore, is the implication it offers that eternal truths expressed in universal themes are available to the ordinary individual who dares to search for them—to look closely within and to observe carefully what lies without. Failing that, others may at least find comfort in the promise of a *time for white roses* that need not be painful but, instead, be a time of spiritual enrichment and optimism, totally devoid of dread and fear.

EPILOGUE

I have a very strong suspicion that the grandchild whose birthday is noted at the end of the "Preface" is a reincarnation of Anamary. I lived with her parents and cared for her while her mother worked from the time she was seven months to a little over two years old. Even after I moved out to my own apartment, I spent a great deal of time with her.

On returning to Pittsburgh from a trip back to Portland once, I brought with me some items from storage there, among them, some of Anamary's aprons. A corner of one was sticking out from a pile of laundry on the floor one day when I was washing at my son's house. Sara passed along by it, stopped, and suddenly said, "That's mine!" She pulled the apron out from among the other things and had me put it on her, and she wore it the rest of the day (with some major adjustments). The pattern and color of the material were unlike those of any of her clothing, so it was definitely not something of her own that she thought she recognized.

Even before she could walk, Sara would crawl to an open drawer or a cabinet door slightly ajar and close them. Her penchant for orderliness that equals Anamary's was certainly not inherited from either of her parents! She is also, even at her age now, the one to whom everyone in her family appeals to learn where items are that cannot be found. Furthermore, the bond between her and me exceeds any natural degree of affection. When she first started talking, she called me "Mommy," and I had to sneak away from the house to go somewhere alone, or she'd scream like a banshee. In the same manner, I was always distraught when Anamary left after her visits to us before she became a resident part of the family. It was like the sundering of souls. Once after her departure, Mother tried to distract me by allowing me to help wash dishes. She offered me the flatwear, which I pushed aside with an indignant "I wanna wash something that'll break!"

A few months before Sara was born, I had a dream which I think was sent to prepare me for Anamary's transition and put everything in perspective. In it I was back at the old home place, where I dunked the baby chickens and spent so many wonderful, magical hours playing in the Big Ditches. Mother and Dad were there, and Anamary too, of course, but dark-haired again and young as she looked at fifty-five. When it was time for me to leave, she said, very typically, that she would walk me to the road.

We picked our way along the half-mile or so of rough lane reduced now, as in the dream, to narrow twin paths in thick, tall weeds. When we got to the foot of the last steep hill, a high brick wall that has never been there loomed before us. To access the road, I had to pass through a huge ornate gate of cast iron that stood wide open.

I hugged Anamary and kissed her goodbye, then stepped out onto the broad, level pavement of what had always been a gravel road. As I did so, the gate swung shut behind me of its own volition, the loud clang sending a terrible pain shooting through my heart. Instantly I knew I would never see this beloved woman again, so I turned, throwing her another kiss, and called back, "I love you!"

"I love you too," she replied, smiling at me through the physical barrier that had intruded itself between us, impassable to me but not to the mutual devotion that would always bind us together. There was no sadness in her demeanor, and no hint of surprise or annoyance.

In the act of setting off once more, I awoke, dragging into consciousness the bittersweet emotions evoked by our parting. As they slowly dissipated, a kind of sublime peace took their place. It seemed clear that my faithful companion—in life *and* in death—had reached out to me in this manner to say that I wouldn't be needing her protection over the rough spots any longer, that the past which had brought me to this juncture in life must now be left in the past. I must detach myself even from her to journey on in true freedom—indeed, relinquish the grip of my ego on all earthly things to which I still clung possessively—and must go forward toward the unknown without fear, specifically that age-old human fear of death, for only without the constrains of fear and desire can anyone be truly free.

Anamary sent me on the wide, smooth highway of my dream secure in the knowledge that a soul traveling with no baggage but love—pure, unselfish, unstinting love—goes far and never travels alone.

Anyone whose interest in reincarnation has been piqued by *A Time for White Roses* is encouraged by the author to read the following books:

Life Cycles: Reincarnation and the Web of Life by Christopher M. Backe, Ph.D.
Reincarnation: an east-west anthology, compiled and edited by Joseph Head and S. L. Cranston
Reincarnation: The Phoenix Fire Mystery, compiled and edited by Head and Cranston
The Case for Reincarnation, by James Dillet Freeman
The Key to Theosophy, by H.P. Blavatsky
To Dance With Angels, by Don and Linda Pendelton

Also highly recommended:

Myths to Live By, by Joseph Campbell
Sacred Science: The King of Pharaonic Theocracy, by R.S. Schwaller de Lubicz

Made in the USA
Lexington, KY
30 July 2018